M000074158

Cream of the Crop

For Deanna –
a friend who is
"the cream of the
crop" in her own
right.

Frank R. Ralph
2005

Copyright © 2005 LeAnn R. Ralph

10-Digit ISBN 1-59113-820-5
13-Digit ISBN 1-59113-820-5

Published by LeAnn R. Ralph, Colfax, Wisconsin, USA.

All rights reserved. No part of this publication may be reproduced, stored in a retrieval system, or transmitted in any form or by any means, electronic, mechanical, recording or otherwise, without the prior written permission of the author.

Printed in the United States of America.

Booklocker.com, Inc.
2005

Cream of the Crop

More True Stories from a Wisconsin Farm

LeAnn R. Ralph

In memory of Tiger Paw Thompson
May 1991 - October 2004

One day I will find you at the Rainbow Bridge.

~~~~~~~~~~~~~~~~~~~~~~~~~~~~~~~~~~

Two cats named Tiger Paw Thompson have come into my life. One was a brown tabby. The other was a silver tabby. The first one, a barn cat born on our dairy farm in west central Wisconsin almost forty years ago, appears in this book in the stories "What's in a Name" and "Chance of Lifetime." The second Tiger Paw Thompson started his life as a barn cat at the stable where I boarded my horses when I lived in southern Wisconsin. His mother, a silver tabby stray who turned out to be a purebred Maine Coon cat, was killed when he was two weeks old, and he and his three siblings, another boy and two girls (Duke, Guinevere and Winifred), came to live with me. The second Tiger Paw Thompson died at 5 a.m. on October 2, 2004, of chronic kidney failure. I shall miss him always.

~~~~~~~~~~~~~~~~~~~~~~~~~~~~~~~~~~

Foreword

In 2004, the owners of the last dairy farm in our neighborhood sold their cows.

I miss seeing the neighbor's Jerseys turned out to pasture. They used to approach the fence when I went for a walk along the dirt road north of my house, curious, as only cows can be curious, smelling like only cows can smell, bringing with them that sweet bovine scent of grass and fresh air and sunshine, sounding like only cows can sound, with the occasional "mooooo!"—the jingle of their neck chains—the gentle scuffle of hooves moving along their cowpaths.

I miss seeing the newborn calves, too, tucked away in a corner of the pasture, waiting for their momma to return from her trip to the barnyard for a drink of water.

And I miss seeing the milk truck go by and waving to the driver if I happened to be outside at that time of day.

Since 1969, Wisconsin has lost 70 percent of its dairy farms and the United States has lost 85 percent. This book is for those who remember the small family dairy farms as I remember them—and for those who will never see a small herd of a dairy cattle grazing peacefully in a green pasture—for those who will never know the wonder of a newborn calf—for those who will never taste 'real' whipped cream as we did in *Cream of the Crop*.

LeAnn R. Ralph
Colfax, Wisconsin

What's In A Name?

From inside the calf pen, four anxious black and white faces watched me through the whitewashed boards. "Maaaaaa!" said one. "Maaaa-AAAA-aaaaaa!" said another. "I know—I know. You're hungry. I'll be there in a minute," I said, as I finished stirring the milk replacer mixture with a paddle Dad had made from a piece of board. I set the paddle in the corner where we kept it when it wasn't being used to stir milk and turned to nudge away the barn cats with the toe of my rubber boot.

"Come on, kitties," I said, "the calves want their supper."

Most of our barn cats were tabbies. Tiger cats we called them. A couple of them were gray. One cat was black, and I had named him Midnight. My mother was superstitious about black cats and would ask me to pick up Midnight if he happened to be on the porch when she was coming out of the house. She said she had a hard enough time as it was, walking around with crutches because of the polio paralysis, and that she did not want a black cat crossing her path. Midnight was a friendly cat who enjoyed winding himself around the closest available ankles—including my mother's—so I picked him up whenever Mom asked me to.

While the calves waited impatiently for their supper, the barn cats, always ready for a quick snack, stood with their front paws on the sides of the calf pails, heads bobbing as they lapped the milk. I tried to push a young tom out of the way, and he turned to look at me but did not take his paws off the bucket.

"Meow!" he said. One eye squinted shut, as if he were winking at me. Then he went back to drinking milk.

"I wish I knew what to call you," I said to the cat.

The tom cat had been born last spring in the haymow. When the kittens were big enough to venture out of the nest, he and his brother and two sisters would chase each other around, up and over and behind the bales, stalking, pouncing, rolling and wrestling. One of their favorite games was 'chase the twine string,' so I would sit on a bale and toss a piece of baler twine, twitching it along the hay and giggling until I had tears in my eyes as the kittens leaped over each other to attack the string. Two of the kittens were tigers and two were white, and right away, I saw that one of the tiger kittens was an expert at using his paws to swat the twine.

After the kittens grew tired of playing, they would crawl into my lap, and as I held them up to my face, I could smell the scent of clover blossoms and alfalfa blossoms in their fur. The whole haymow smelled like clover and alfalfa and made me think of hot summer days and bright blue skies and the sound of the baler working its way up and down the windrows—*ka-chink, ka-chink, ka-chink, trippa-trippa-trip, ka-chink, ka-chink, ka-chink.*

When the kittens were old enough to leave their mother, I gave the two white ones to our elderly neighbor, Hannah Paulson, because she said they reminded her of a white cat she'd had when she was a little girl. Hannah had named the white kittens Snowflake and Snowball. The other tiger kitten had two white spots, one on her chest the size of a dime and one on the tip of her toe, so I called her Tippy.

But none of the names I tried for the kitten that was good at using his paws had seemed quite right. He wasn't a Skippy or a Happy or a Lucky, and he wasn't a Frank or a Christopher or a Henry. Finally I gave in and called him Tommy, which is what Dad called all of our tom cats. No matter what I had named a boy cat, Dad would call him Tommy. Even Midnight.

"Okay, kitties, I gotta feed the calves," I said, as I leaned down to pick up two of the pails.

The young tabby tom was not going to give up that easily. When I lifted the pail, he hung on and hooked his claws over the edge. I wouldn't have thought a cat could hang onto a pail, but this one could. I set both pails on the floor, and, using two hands, one to hold the paw and the other to lift the claws off the rim, broke his grip on the bucket. The cat looked up at me with an accusing expression in his green-gold eyes, as if to say, "what did you do that for?" I picked up the cat and held him against my shoulder. "I know you like to drink out of the pail," I said, "but I have to feed the calves." The tabby tom rested his head on my arm. He was purring. I could not hear him over the sound of the milker pump and the swish-swish of the vacuum lines, but I knew he was purring because I could feel his body trembling. I had picked up enough purring cats to know purring when I felt it.

"Don't worry. You'll get more milk in your dish later," I said. I set the cat on the floor and leaned down again to pick up two of the pails.

Dad and my big brother, Ingman, were almost finished milking. Three cows were left to milk on each side of the barn, but my father said the calves should drink their milk before he finished with the cows so that by the time he was ready to feed hay, the calves would be ready to eat hay. At such a young age, the calves were not eating much hay, but it was enough to make it worthwhile to give them some. That's what Dad said, anyway.

I turned toward the calf pen, a pail in each hand. "Maaaaa-aaaaa!!" said the calves, all four at once.

Ever since I was big enough and strong enough to carry a pail of milk, it had been my job to feed the calves. Feeding the calves was easy. All you had to do was set the buckets in the mangers, and the calves would do the rest.

Except that right now, feeding the calves was not quite so easy.

Four calves lived in the pen—but I only had two hands. And I knew the calves would fight over the pails until I could bring the other two, and in the meantime, one pail, or both, might be spilled in the calf manger. Dad never said much when the calves spilled their milk, although I knew he didn't like it. For one thing, the milk was wasted, and for another thing, spilled milk made a terrible mess in the manger.

"I'll carry the other pails if you want me to," said my big brother, Ingman.

Sometimes the kids at school asked me about Ingman's name. My big brother is twenty-one years older than me. Mom said he was named after her Norwegian mother, Inga, and that the name 'Ingman' is a masculine form of the name 'Inga.' I have a big sister, too. Her name is Loretta, and she is nineteen years older than me. Our mother was stricken with polio when she was twenty-six and partially paralyzed in both legs, and after the polio, the doctors told her she would never have more children. I was born sixteen years later when Mom was forty-two.

I turned to look at my big brother, who had stepped into the center aisle and was walking toward me, his black rubber chore boots scuffling against the white barn lime Dad had sprinkled on the floor.

"Would you really carry the other two pails for me?" I asked.

"Sure," he said, giving me a sly sidelong glance. "Anything for my *baby* sister!"

To my way of thinking, it wasn't especially nice for Ingman to call me a baby. Mom thought otherwise. "He was a grown man when you were born! Of *course* you are his baby sister," she had said one time when I mentioned it.

Ingman worked at the creamery in town six miles away. This week he was working the 7-to-3 shift, so he was able to be in the barn for the evening milking. He picked up the remaining two pails, and when we approached the pen, the calves scrambled for position along the manger where we fed them. They were in such a hurry to get their supper that they kept bumping into each other.

Our barn had three calf pens, but so early in the fall, the other two were empty. Later on, after more calves were born, all three pens would be full for a while until Dad decided which calves he wanted to keep and which ones he was going to sell.

As I stepped across the gutter channel, the young brown tabby tom trotted ahead of me. Suddenly, the cat stopped, crouched and leaped from the floor to the top board of the calf pen. He landed lightly on his feet and turned to look at us.

I couldn't believe how fast he had jumped. One second he was on the floor. The next second he was on the calf pen.

"Hi-ya kitty," Ingman said.

The calves strained forward eagerly, their knees hitting the side of the pen with a dull thudding sound. We set the pails in the manger, but the calves couldn't seem to get their noses into the buckets fast enough, and two of them started drinking out of the same pail. Ingman grabbed one calf by the ear and directed her to the other pail.

The calves settled down to drinking, and while we stood there watching them, my brother patted the tom cat, who closed his eyes and rubbed his head against Ingman's hand.

The little Holsteins made quick work of the milk—with a whole lot of slurping, guzzling, and sipping noises thrown in for good measure— and soon began to rattle their buckets. Most of our cows were Holsteins, although we also had a couple of Guernseys and a Jersey.

I leaned over to hold the edge of one pail so the calf wouldn't spill the rest of the milk. A long time ago, I had learned that if someone didn't tilt the calf pails and hold them, the calves would tip the buckets over trying to lick up every last drop.

Another calf reached the bottom of the pail, so Ingman leaned over to tip it sideways for her. At the same time, the young tom cat reached down with one paw and touched the top of Ingman's head.

My brother glanced up.

The cat sat straight and still, looking as though he hadn't moved a muscle in the last five minutes.

"Did you do that?" Ingman asked, turning toward me.

"Do what?" I said.

"Touch me on the head?"

"Why would I touch you on the head?"

Ingman shrugged and reached down to tip another pail.

I put my hand over my mouth so I wouldn't laugh out loud as once again, the cat extended his paw. When the paw was about to touch my brother's head, Ingman glanced up again. "Hah!" he said. "It *was* you!"

The cat withdrew and squinted his eyes at my big brother, as if to say, "Yes, I guess you caught me, didn't you."

After the calves were finished and we had removed the pails from the manger, Ingman cleaned wet hay from the watering cup. The calves rooted around in their hay, like the cows did, and they often flipped some of it into their water. To me, the watering cups looked like upside-down army helmets.

As my brother bent over the watering cup, once again the cat stretched out his paw, and this time, it rested on top of Ingman's head.

"You like using that paw, don't you," Ingman commented, looking up at the cat.

The cat hesitated and then gently patted my brother's nose, in much the same way that my mother used her finger to pat a cake in the oven to see if it was finished baking.

"Good thing he didn't use his claws!" I said.

I knew all about the barn cats and their claws. I had watched them sharpen their claws on the posts of the calf pen, dangerous-looking white hooks extended, digging into the wood, until in places, the posts were shredded and ragged and splintered. Sometimes, too, the cats would put their paws on my leg when I was ready to carry a pail of milk to the milkhouse and they were waiting for me to dump more milk in their dish. A few of them liked to flex their claws into my chore pants—and also into my skin, which is why I often walked around with pin-prick puncture wounds on my legs.

Ingman grinned, showing his very white and very even teeth. "Yeah, good thing he didn't use his claws," he replied. "Otherwise, I probably wouldn't have a nose left."

Now that the calves had finished their supper, I stacked the four pails together and carried them to the faucet on the other side of the barn. Ingman went back to milking. As I rinsed the pails, I looked toward the calf pen and saw that the young tabby tom was washing his face by licking his front paw and swiping it over his ears, licking his paw and swiping it over his ears. He stopped, leaned down to clean his tail, and then went back to washing his face. Dad said cats liked to groom when they were happy and contented.

The next evening when I was ready to feed calves, Ingman once again helped me carry the buckets to the manger.

"Where's our friend?" he asked.

"Friend? What friend?"

"Tiger Paw Thompson," my brother replied.

"Tiger WHO?"

"Paw Thompson," Ingman said.

Tiger Paw Thompson?

Just then, the young tabby tom cat from the evening before jumped on the calf pen, sat down and began grooming.

"There's Tiger Paw Thompson!" Ingman exclaimed.

The cat paused in scrubbing his face and held out one front paw, toes spread apart as if he were reaching for something.

"Pleased to meet you," Ingman said, grasping the small striped paw in his large, muscular hand.

I looked at the cat, sitting there on the calf pen with his paw in Ingman's hand.

Then I looked at my big brother, who had leaned forward and was almost nose-to-nose with the cat.

Wouldn't you just know it.

I had tried and tried and *tried* to think of something to call the cat, but then, just like that, Ingman had found the perfect name.

All at once, my stomach felt hollow. I was the one who had played with the tabby cat when he was a kitten. I was the one who picked him up and held him and petted him. And I was the one who had worried about him when he limped around for several days after a calf had stepped on his toes.

"How come I didn't get to name him?" I blurted out.

"What?" Ingman said.

"How come I didn't get to name the cat?"

"What do you mean, how come you didn't get to name the cat. What do you *want* to call him?" Ingman asked.

The hollow feeling in my stomach inched its way up into my throat.

"I tried and tried to think of a good name, but I couldn't find one," I said.

"We don't have to call him Tiger Paw Thompson, you know," Ingman replied.

I was tempted to tell my big brother that I wanted to find a name for the cat all by myself—until I remembered the names I had already tried. The truth of the matter was that none of those names had been anywhere close to as good as this one.

"But Tiger Paw Thompson is a really, really good name," I said. "How did you ever think of it?"

"Well," my brother said, "he's a tiger cat, he likes to use his paw, and he's a tom cat. Put 'em all together, and you've got…"

"Tiger Paw Thompson," I said.

I reached up and petted the top of the cat's head, tracing the tabby stripes between his ears and the stripes marking the side of his face. "Hi Tiger Paw Thompson!"

The cat stared at me with his green-gold eyes, and then his jaws snapped open in a wide yawn. "Meow!" he said.

"Hey!" I exclaimed. "I think he already knows his name!"

From the center aisle came the sound of a thump accompanied by the clinking and clanking of stainless steel milker inflations. Dad had finished milking one cow and was ready to move to the next one. He placed the cover on an empty milker bucket, latched the handle and turned toward us. Dad smiled when he saw the cat sitting on the calf pen.

"Is Tommy helping you feed the calves?" my father asked as he stepped across the gutter channel.

"His name isn't Tommy," I said.

"Well, I don't know what you've been calling him, but that's what I call him," Dad replied.

"His name," I continued, "is Tiger Paw Thompson."

Dad's sky blue eyes widened. "Tiger *what?*" he asked.

"Paw Thompson," Ingman responded.

The cat looked at Dad and then stretched out his paw.

"What's the paw for?" Dad asked as he stroked the tiger-striped head.

Tiger Paw Thompson put his paw on Dad's hand.

"It just hit me all of a sudden," Ingman explained, "that his name is Tiger Paw Thompson."

"Hmmmm," Dad replied. "I guess that *is* a good name for him. The last couple of days he's been sitting on the calf pen when I've been carrying feed. And every time I walk past, he holds out that paw of his."

Ingman caught my eye and grinned.

"So," Dad said, as he lifted off his blue-and-white pin-striped chore cap and settled it back on his head, "I guess that means you're not Tommy anymore, are you."

After that, Tiger Paw Thompson would sit on the calf pen in the morning and during the evening so he could gently pat the heads, faces or shoulders of anyone who came within his reach. As time passed, he grew to be a large, well-muscled tom and developed into a fierce hunter who killed mice, rats, pocket gophers, chipmunks and the occasional snake that ventured into the pole shed.

In spite of his reputation as a hunter, Tiger Paw Thompson often put his paws on my leg and begged to be picked up, although unlike the other cats, he never flexed his claws. He either hung over my shoulder or else I would hold him in my arms as I wandered around the buildings looking for Dad, or while I waited to carry milk, or sometimes on my way to the house. Dad said he had never seen a cat who liked to be carried around as much as Tiger Paw Thompson.

I never did quite get over it, though.

For once we had a tom cat that Dad called by his rightful name.

Why couldn't I have been the one to think of it?

****

2

A Trip To Hawaii

When the bus finally stopped at the foot of our driveway, I jumped down the steps and ran all the way up the hill. I was in such a hurry that I barely noticed the wild plums growing next to the spring, although on any other day, I would have stopped to pick some. Every September, the twisted, crooked branches became heavy with small, round rosy-red plums. The yellow plum pulp was tart, but the juice was one of the sweetest things I had ever tasted. Even when my mother was a little girl, clumps of plum brush had been growing by the spring that ran next to the driveway.

I reached the willow tree, took a shortcut, scrambled up the bank and trotted across the lawn, up the concrete steps and into the porch.

"Mom!" I shouted, letting the door slam behind me. I threw my books on the kitchen table and rushed into the living room. "Mom!"

My mother looked up from her embroidery. For the past few months, she had been working on items for the church bazaar that would be held later this fall, and she was now working on a dresser scarf. Mom said that since she couldn't do much else because of the polio, she might as well make things the church could sell.

"What's wrong?" my mother asked, reaching for the scissors so she could snip off a piece of blue thread.

"Guess what?!" I said.

I flopped down on the couch and didn't bother waiting for my mother to politely ask "what?" before telling her my big news.

"We're studying Hawaii in school! Can I go see Mrs. Paulson?"

Hannah Paulson, our elderly next-door neighbor, was a retired kindergarten teacher who had taught in Seattle. Several years earlier, she and her husband, Bill, who had bought the farm below our driveway from a relative of Mrs. Paulson's, had taken a trip to Hawaii.

My mother frowned as she threaded the embroidery needle. "You want to visit Mrs. Paulson? Right now?"

"Yes," I said, nodding so hard that my blond bangs bounced up and down on my forehead.

"Can't it wait until this weekend?" Mom asked, using her thumb and forefinger to tie a knot in the end of the floss.

I shook my head. During the school year I was allowed to visit Hannah only on Saturdays.

"I have to go now because I want to ask her if I can borrow some of her things from Hawaii," I explained. "So I can take them to school."

My mother's frown deepened, and I knew I was coming to the tricky part. I was pretty sure Hannah would allow me to borrow a few of her keepsakes, but getting my mother to agree to let me ask was a different story all together.

"You know how I feel about borrowing," Mom began.

"Please, Mom? Pleeeeease? This will be my one and only chance—"

"For what?" my mother interrupted.

Although we did not have regular show-and-tell sessions in my elementary school class, not like we did when we were little kids in kindergarten, the teacher said we could still bring something to school if we wanted to.

"This will be my chance to bring something for show-and-tell from another state," I explained. "Some of the other kids go on trips to Florida or Disneyland. Or they visit relatives down south. But I never have things like that. And nobody's been to Hawaii..."

I also knew for certain we were never going to go to Hawaii. Our family did not go on vacations. Dad said he had too much work to do, and Mom said she couldn't get around well enough to go 'gallivanting' as she called it.

I had always thought bringing something from another state must be tremendous fun. One time a boy had brought an orange from Florida after they had gone on a trip during Christmas vacation. It was the biggest orange I had ever seen. Bigger than *any* of us had ever seen.

But, to tell the truth, the kids who brought items for show-and-tell from vacations were not farmers. Farm kids, I had noticed, were more likely to bring deer antlers they had found in the woods. Or one of those huge, gray wasp nests (without the wasps). And once a boy had brought in a cow's eye. Lightning had killed the poor animal during a fall thunderstorm, and the boy's dad figured it would be a useful item for our science class. Which it was. Even though none of the girls wanted to touch it. But I'd never had anything like that to bring to class, either, so I was not about to let go of my one and only chance to bring something from Hawaii.

"Mom?" I said. "Can't I please just *find out* if she would let me borrow something?"

My mother's face softened. "Well… maybe…I guess…"

She looked at me sternly and held up one forefinger. "But only if you promise—"

"Yes!" I broke in. "I promise to say please. And to be very careful with what I borrow. If Hannah lets me borrow anything, that is. And if she says no, I won't pester her about it. Cross my heart."

My mother sighed. "Oh, all right, then. But don't stay too long. It'll be suppertime soon."

I usually ate a snack when I came home from school, but today, I forgot all about it, and a few minutes later, I found myself standing in Mrs. Paulson's living room, clutching a folded paper grocery bag Mom said I could take with me just in case.

I told Hannah we were studying Hawaii in school. She smiled and turned to open the drawer of her china cabinet. Out came a paper bag of seashells she had collected during their vacation to Hawaii. One exceptionally large shell was white and spiny on the outside and a smooth, pale, delicate pink on the inside.

"This is called a conch shell, and if you hold it up to your ear, you can hear the sound of the ocean," she said.

I put the shell to my ear and was surprised at how cold and heavy it felt. And then, much to my amazement, I heard a faint sound like rushing water.

"You really can hear the ocean!" I exclaimed, handing the shell back to my neighbor.

Hannah put the shell up to her ear. "I had forgotten how soothing that sound is," she said as she set the conch shell on the coffee table.

In the light of late afternoon, the coffee table's dark polished surface reflected back the image of the white conch shell. We didn't have a coffee table at home. I wished we did, because then I could sit on the floor by it and have a writing table handy for doing my homework. I could also use it as a place to leave the latest book I was reading, instead of going all the way upstairs to my room to get a book if I wanted to read. And I could maybe even use a coffee table as a place to eat snacks, although that seemed rather unlikely since Mom frowned on eating in the living room.

Hannah turned to the china cabinet and reached into the drawer again. After the seashells, I wasn't sure what to expect. This time she produced a stack of postcards.

"If you look on the back," Hannah explained, "there's a little paragraph telling about the picture."

The first postcard showed a pretty young woman with long dark hair. She wore an off-the-shoulder white dress and a big necklace made of bright pink flowers. In school we had learned that a flower necklace from Hawaii was called a lei. I turned over the postcard and found out something else about the flower necklaces. "Tradition says that if a visitor tosses a lei into the ocean and it floats back to shore, then one day, the visitor will return to Hawaii," the postcard said.

Mrs. Paulson reached into the drawer again, and this time she brought out a small photo album and handed it to me. I opened the front cover, and the first picture was of Hannah and Bill standing beneath a palm tree. Hannah wore a long bright blue dress decorated with big white flowers; Bill was wearing an ordinary white button-down short-sleeved shirt. Bill, with his thick bifocal glasses and gray crew cut hair, was not the type who would wear Hawaiian shirts. Hannah and Bill were, however, each wearing a lei made of pink and white flowers.

"Did you throw your leis into the ocean?" I asked.

Hannah shook her head. "No, actually, we didn't. I thought they were much too pretty to throw them into the water."

Mrs. Paulson placed the seashells, postcards and the photo album into the paper grocery bag I had brought along and handed it to me.

I could hardly believe it. The seashells would have been enough. But all three? Seashells, postcards *and* pictures!

Hannah then opened the china cabinet door and took out a small paper sack. As she withdrew her hand from the sack, I almost forgot to take my next breath.

Mrs. Paulson was holding a long necklace made of tiny, dark brown, polished seeds strung together in intricate patterns. I had always loved that necklace. The first time Hannah showed it to me, she explained how the seeds had been sewn together by hand. "It took someone a very long time to make that necklace, so that's why I keep it in the china cabinet. I don't want it to get broken," she had said.

Hannah carefully put the necklace back into the small paper bag and folded over the top. Then she placed the little bag inside the bigger bag that I was still holding by its waxed string handles.

I opened my mouth a couple of times but no words came out.

"Are...are...you sure...you want to let me take the necklace?" I asked in a squeaky voice.

"I'm sure," Hannah said. "Finding it was one the best parts of the trip."

I drew a deep breath and let it out slowly.

"I promise I will be really, *really*, REALLY careful with all of it," I said.

Mrs. Paulson smiled, the corners of her eyes crinkling behind the wire-rimmed glasses she wore.

"I know you'll be careful," Hannah said.

As if the sea shells, postcards, pictures and the necklace were not enough, Hannah went on to make another suggestion that was so astounding, I almost dropped the grocery bag.

"You know," Mrs. Paulson said, "I have a whole box of slides from that trip. Would you like me to come to class, show the slides and talk about Hawaii, too?"

I stared at Hannah, dumbfounded. My mouth popped open, but since I didn't know what to say, I shut it again.

She laughed. "I will assume that's a 'yes.' Tomorrow I will call your teacher so we can set up a time."

A little while later on the way home with the paper bag bumping against my leg, I felt like I was dreaming.

Other kids had brought in objects for show-and-tell—which I was now going to do, too—but so far, no one had brought a real, live person.

The next day, my classmates took turns holding the conch shell up to their ears and crowding around the library table at the back of the room to look at the pictures, postcards and other seashells.

The only thing missing from the library table was the seed necklace. My teacher told me to carry the necklace around to each desk so the other students could see it. Then she put the necklace back in the small paper bag and it stayed in her desk drawer until it was time to go home.

When I told my classmates that my neighbor was coming to school pretty soon so she could to tell us about Hawaii, some of them didn't believe me.

"She'll be here. You'll see," I said.

Mrs. Paulson came to class a few days later wearing a navy skirt and jacket and a pale pink blouse. Hannah wore short-sleeved shirtwaist dresses at home, and often with an apron tied around her waist, although when I saw her at church—the little white country church a half mile from our farm—Hannah wore tailored dresses and sometimes a hat to match.

Our teacher helped Mrs. Paulson set up the slide projector, and then she pulled the white screen down over the blackboard, turned off the lights, and suddenly, almost larger than life, were tall palm trees and beds filled with flowers unlike anything I had ever seen before.

As Hannah showed us the slides, she told all about where they had been and what they had seen and done, such as the luau where they had eaten roast pig. "There was so much food at the luau that we could only take a small sample of everything," she said, "and even at that, it was more food than we were used to eating."

Other slides were of the hotel overlooking the ocean where they had stayed. "We kept the sliding door open all night so we could hear the sound of the waves," Hannah told us.

And then there was the shop where she had purchased the seed necklace. "It was a tiny, little gift shop on a back street. The shop owner told me it had taken a very long time to sew those seeds together," Mrs. Paulson explained.

The last slide clicked off the screen at the front of the room, and our teacher turned on the lights. Mrs. Paulson walked to the teacher's desk and picked up a brown paper bag that she had left sitting on the floor.

"Now I have a surprise for you," she said. "Can anyone guess what it is?"

As the minutes ticked away, the guesses became more and more wild. Some of my classmates thought maybe she had brought a lei and others thought she had a real Hawaiian muumuu to show us. One boy said he had read in a book that Hawaii didn't have any snakes, except for tropical sea snakes, and that maybe she had a tropical sea snake in the bag.

"Young man, if there was a sea snake in this bag—or any other kind of snake—I would not be in the same building with it, much less the same room," Hannah declared.

The boy grinned. "My mom doesn't like snakes, either. That's why she won't let me bring them in the house."

Mrs. Paulson smiled back at him. "I think your mother must be a very wise woman."

Hannah reached inside the brown paper bag. She pulled her hand back, and out came a pineapple. A real, fresh, whole pineapple. But it wasn't one pineapple. It was two. And that wasn't all she had in the shopping bag. Next came two coconuts.

"Where did you get those?" one girl asked. "Did you bring them back from Hawaii?"

Hannah shook her head. "No. They wouldn't have kept this long. I got them at the grocery store."

"Here?" another of my classmates asked. "In town?"

"Oh, no," Hannah said. "I had to drive a long ways to get them."

"Minneapolis?" asked one girl. "Sometimes my mom goes to Minneapolis to visit friends. She says they have GREAT BIG grocery stores there."

Mrs. Paulson shook her head. "No. I didn't have to go *that* far."

Hannah asked us to come up by rows so we could look at the pineapple and the coconut and touch them and hold them. Sometimes we had canned pineapple at home that my mother put in pineapple upside-down cake. But I had never seen a whole pineapple before. The pineapple felt prickly—a little like a cucumber, I thought.

The oblong brown coconut felt as hard as the rocks Dad picked out of the back field when he plowed in the spring and had short, wiry fibers all over it that felt like the twine strings which held our hay bales together at home. The top of the coconut had what looked like two round eyes and a mouth. Mrs. Paulson said the round spots were where the coconut had been attached to the palm tree.

Once we'd all had a chance to touch the pineapple and the coconut, Mrs. Paulson used a knife to trim off the prickly part of the pineapples and to cut them into slices. She had also brought little white paper plates and white paper napkins for us.

While we ate the pineapple, our teacher left the room to find one of the janitors, who used a nail to poke two holes in the top of the coconuts to drain out the white liquid that Hannah said was called coconut milk. Then he took the hammer and broke the coconuts into pieces. The coconut pieces smelled like the coconut Mom bought at the store for baking. But unlike the shredded coconut, which came in a plastic bag and was soft and easy to eat, the fresh coconut chunks were hard and very chewy.

Just as we finished our 'Wisconsin luau,' as Hannah called it, the bell rang for afternoon recess. While the other kids filed out of the room, I stayed behind.

"Did I do a good job?" Mrs. Paulson asked.

"It was the very, very bestest job in the whole wide world," I said. "Oh—and I *almost* forgot. Mom said I should be sure to say thank you."

Hannah smiled and plucked a piece of lint off the sleeve of her navy blue suit. "You already said thank you when the whole class did," she said.

I lifted one shoulder in a slight shrug. "I know. But Mom said I should say a special one, because…"

"What?" Mrs. Paulson asked.

"Because she said the sea shells and the postcards and the pictures and the necklace were more than enough already."

Mrs. Paulson picked up the stack of used paper plates and put them into the waste basket. "Do you know that *you* did *me* a favor?"

My eyebrows drew together in a frown. "I did?"

"Since I retired, I've missed teaching, and I have especially missed being around students. This was like old times," Hannah said.

"It was?"

"Yes. So, tell your mom that you remembered the special thank you, and that I said I enjoyed it as much as the class did. All right?"

The next day, the other kids kept talking about Mrs. Paulson's visit to school and how much fun it had been, and how nice she was, and how they had never expected to eat pineapple and coconut.

Okay, so maybe I hadn't brought anything from a vacation that I had taken with my family. But thanks to Hannah, my most perfect show-and-tell ever was positively the next-best thing.

****

3

Old Habits Die Hard

One October afternoon as I shifted my books to the other arm and started up the hill toward the house, cows were the farthest thing from my mind. The sky was color of the turquoise dress my mother liked to wear to church, and the air—filled with the scent of old leaves, ripe wild grapes growing in the fenceline and plums that had fallen to the ground and split open—felt so warm that if I didn't know better, I would think it was summer. Dad said at this time of year nice weather would not last long, and in another month, we might have snow on the ground. We hadn't had weather this nice in more than a week, and I wanted to ride Dusty, my plump brown pony with the white mane and tail. That is, I wanted to ride Dusty if Mom would give me permission. Sometimes my mother had chores she wanted me to do as soon as I got home from school.

At the halfway point up the hill of our driveway, just beyond the plum trees growing in the fenceline, I could see Dusty, grazing on the sidehill in her pasture. The grass was not as green as it had been in the spring and summer, but as far as Dusty was concerned, grass was grass, even if it was faded grass and not growing much anymore. My pony spent so much time nibbling grass in her pasture that in most places, except for the spots where she had left piles of manure and did not want to eat the grass there, her pasture was shorter than the grass in the lawn. My big sister said she ought to mow the lawn again before winter, but so far, she hadn't gotten around to it, although maybe that was because Dad had told her the grass would come back better next spring if it was not cut short this fall.

"Hi Dusty!" I shouted.

The pony threw her head up, stared at me, and then trotted toward the fence, ears perked, nickering. Beneath her feet, the yellow leaves of the silver maples growing along the edge of the yard, which had dropped half their leaves on the lawn and half in the pasture, made a swishing, crunching sound.

I looked toward the house and saw my mother sitting in her chair by the picture window. She was holding the newspaper up in front of her but was gazing directly back at me. She let one corner of the newspaper drop and waved. I waved back, and then I climbed the bank and headed across the lawn toward the porch steps. Yellow leaves from the silver maple not far from the living room window covered the lawn, and while I shuffled my way through the leaves, Dusty watched me from the other side of the fence. She knew I was going into the house, so she put her nose to the ground and went back to picking grass.

"Boy, am I glad you're home," Mom called out from the living room as the screen door latched shut behind me.

A sinking feeling settled in the pit of my stomach. "Why?" I said.

Whenever my mother informed me that she was glad I was home, she usually had something she wanted me to do.

"I'm glad you're home because Dad started picking corn today, so I want you to put the cows in and feed them," she said.

I set my books on the kitchen table and went into the living room.

"Me? You want me to put the cows in? All by myself?"

Once in early spring when Dad had gone sucker fishing, my sister had helped me put the cows in the barn because, at the time, we had a bull, and Mom did not want me to put the cows in alone. The bull, a friendly yearling we called Bully-Loo, had since grown up and had been sold a while back. And during summer vacation, I had put the cows in by myself several times, but that was when we didn't have any heifers. Over the summer, three Holstein heifers had grown big enough so they could go into stanchions, and every evening for the past week, it had taken both Dad and I to get them into the barn.

All summer long, my father had fed the heifers in a feed trough he had built in the barnyard. Last spring, the heifers were not big enough to go into stanchions, but they were too big to stay in the calf pen. Well, it wasn't that they were *too* big to stay in the calf pen if one of them had gone in one pen and two in the other pen, except they were such good friends, they all three wanted to be in the same pen together. Dad figured if they stayed outside for the summer, he would not have to clean calf pens, and so, he had built the feed trough in the barnyard.

The heifers had quickly caught onto the idea that when the cows went into the barn, they should stand by the feed trough and wait for someone to bring out a pail of feed. But as Dad and I had discovered right away last week, the heifers would rather stand by the feed trough than come into the barn. My father said they did not want to come inside to eat because they were used to eating their feed outside. 'Old habits die hard' is what he'd said. When I asked him what that meant, he said it meant habits are hard to break and it would take a while for the heifers to become accustomed to the routine of eating in the barn.

"Did Dad say I should put the cows in?" I asked.

Mom shook her head. "No, but if you put them in this time, then for as long as the weather holds, your father can stay out in the field later and still start milking when he usually does."

I knew what she was getting at. If I put the cows in, then Dad would have an extra hour every day to pick corn and would finish that much sooner.

"But what about the heifers?" I asked.

My mother pulled off her black-rimmed reading glasses and folded them up. "What about the heifers?"

"They're hard to get in," I said.

"Oh, don't be silly. Those heifers have been going into the barn for a week. They ought to be used to it by now."

Easy for Mom to think the heifers should be used to going into the barn. My mother had been paralyzed by polio before I was born and couldn't get around well enough to put cows in the barn.

"I know it's been a long time since I've been able to do chores," Mom continued, "although I don't think heifers are so very much different nowadays."

"But Mom—they don't like to come in the barn."

My mother shook her head and frowned. "Nonsense. When they see the other cows going into the stanchions, they will go in, too," she said.

I knew better than to try to change her mind.

I also knew I would probably still be chasing those heifers around the barnyard when Dad came home.

I went upstairs to change out of my school clothes and stood for a minute by the bedroom window, looking at the bright October sunshine. By the time I finished putting the cows in the barn—if I could even get the heifers in—it would be suppertime. So much for riding Dusty today. Or on any other day for the rest of the week.

A little while later, I headed to the barn to measure feed for the cows. I worked my way down one row of stanchions and back up the other side, placing two scoops of feed in front of each stanchion. I could hear the cows moving around in the barnyard on the concrete slab in front of the door. The cows knew I was measuring out feed, and each of them wanted to be the first one inside.

Even though the air was cooler here in the barn, big, fat, black flies bumped and buzzed against the windowpanes, taking advantage of the sunshine streaming through the south windows. In a few weeks, when the weather turned cold, the flies would find someplace warm to hide for the winter.

I finished dumping the feed, opened the door and moved back out of the way as one by one, the cows rushed toward their stanchions. Their hooves went clickety-clack along the barn aisle, and some of them were in such a hurry, they were practically trotting toward their stalls.

When the last cow had come into the barn, I walked out the door and saw the three heifers standing next to the feed trough on the other side of the barnyard, tails swishing back and forth to chase away the flies.

Over the past week, my father and I had invented a system for getting the heifers in the barn. Dad would take a pail of cow feed (a mixture of ground corn and oats and molasses) and coax them away from the trough while I walked along behind them, waving my arms. Bit by bit we would move them toward the barn, and when they were safely inside, I would shut the door to keep them from going back into the barnyard. Then, once the heifers were in the barn, while Dad continued to coax them forward, I stayed behind them until they went into their stalls.

I stood on the concrete slab, looking at the heifers and wondering how I was going to get them into the barn by myself, until I remembered all of a sudden that I had not yet shut the stanchions. I turned and went inside the barn where the cows were busy eating their feed. At this time of year, the summer birds were gone, and something seemed out of place without the happy chatter of the barn swallows.

I stepped across the gutter channel and walked along in front of the cows to shut each stanchion. In our barn, the cows faced the wall, although Dad said some barns were the other way, with the cows facing the center aisle and their tails toward the wall. The wood-and-metal stanchions were easy to shut on this side of the barn because the cows had only started to eat their feed and were not pushing forward, but I knew that when I reached the end of the barn on the other side, shutting the stanchions would be harder since some of the cows would be stretching to reach more of their feed or to swipe some from their next-door neighbor.

I soon saw that I was right about the cows on the other end of the barn and spent a few minutes convincing some of them to move back a step or two so I could close their stanchions. I wanted to be sure the stanchions were firmly latched because if a stanchion popped open and the cow went outside again after she was finished eating her feed, she would not want to come back in the barn. This had happened once or twice while I was helping Dad put the cows in.

Satisfied that all of the stanchions were firmly latched, I went to the feed box, put some cow feed into a pail and headed for the barnyard. As soon as I stepped out of the door onto the concrete slab, the heifers, who had been watching for me, turned toward the feed trough. I took a better grip on the handle of the feed pail and set off across the barnyard. As I made my way toward the heifers, I kept a sharp eye on the ground in front of me so I wouldn't accidentally step in a cow pie. Dry cow manure wasn't so bad, but fresh cow pies were downright soupy, and I did not want to have to stop, go to the milkhouse and clean off my shoes with the hose.

The closer I came to the heifers, the more they crowded around the feed trough. One heifer pushed another one out of her way by putting her head down and nudging the other heifer's flank.

I knew what the heifers were thinking.

"I'm not dumping this out here. You have to come in the barn," I said.

One of the heifers, the one that had pushed her companion, turned her head and looked at me with soft, friendly eyes. She was mostly black with a little white spot on her forehead and two white feet. Some of our Holsteins were jumpy and nervous, but the three heifers were used to seeing people, and they knew that a person with a pail meant they would get something good to eat.

"Come bossie," I said. "Come bossie, come bossie."

I wasn't sure why I was saying 'come bossie, come bossie.' What was I going to do after that? If I backed my way toward the barn, would the heifers follow?

Holding the pail out in front of me, I started backing toward the barn. I couldn't go very fast, since I had to keep looking down to see what was on the ground behind me, and at this rate, I knew the trip to the barn was going to take a long time.

"Come bossie, come bossie," I said, looking back at the heifers again.

I was so certain the heifers would not come away from the feed trough that I nearly dropped the pail when all three began to follow me.

I backed across the barnyard, alternating between keeping a watchful eye on the ground behind me, and a watchful eye on the heifers in front of me, and wondered what I was going to do once I reached the barn. I knew I could not circle around and shut the door, because if I did, the heifers would follow me outside. The object was to bring them *into* the barn—not to let them outside again.

Although, now that I had plenty of time to think during my slow backward walk across the barnyard, maybe I wouldn't have to shut the door. Maybe Mom was right. The heifers *had* been going into the barn for one whole week.

Many minutes later, I backed through the barn door, with the heifers still following. They reminded me of kittens following their mother when she is taking them out to teach them how to hunt. I had seen the barn cats numerous times, headed across the barnyard with their kittens following single file behind them.

After I got into the barn, I kept right on shaking the pail, and the heifers kept right on following me.

Wouldn't it be something if, after a week of Dad and I trying to get the heifers into the barn, that tonight, when I was putting them in for the first time by myself, they went into their stalls? Dad would be *so* surprised when he came home.

I still hadn't figured out one thing, though. How was I going to persuade the heifers to go into their stanchions?

I was almost to the first empty stanchion when an idea came to me. Maybe, if I backed into the stall so the heifers could still see the pail of feed, one of them would follow me, and then, I could back through the middle of the stanchion, and when the heifer put her head into the stanchion, I could close it, and then I could do the same with the other two.

I stopped to let the heifers catch up.

"Here," I said, "Look what I've got."

Dad never let the heifers eat out of the pail when he was in the barnyard, coaxing them into the barn, because he said he didn't want them to think that maybe he was going to feed them outside. But once he got into the barn, Dad often let the heifers eat a bite of feed as a reward for following him.

The heifers knew what to do when the bucket was held toward them, and each one was more than willing to put her nose into the pail and eat some cow feed.

So far—so good.

Glancing behind me to avoid stepping off the edge of the concrete, I backed over the gutter channel, chanting "come-bossie, come-bossie, come-bossie, come-bossie."

When my back was almost against the wood and metal stanchion, the mostly-black heifer took a step over the gutter and began to follow me into the stall.

I wanted to yell "yipee!" but decided I had better keep quiet. I did not want to scare the heifers.

Still, I couldn't keep from smiling to myself. This was going to work out all—

I didn't even get a chance to think the word 'right.'

With a startled "Moooo-oooo!" the heifer, standing with only her front feet in the stall, whirled around and leaped into the center aisle. She bumped into her companions and then pushed past them. One heifer, reeling from the collision, nearly fell into the gutter channel, but, fortunately, regained her footing and got back into the center aisle before the cow in the stanchion in front of her could react. Some of our cows were awfully quick with their feet. That's what Dad said—they were 'awfully quick with their feet'—and the cow in front of the heifer who had stepped into the gutter was one of those who could kick in the blink of an eye.

Before I quite knew what was happening, all three of the heifers had turned and were running toward the door at the far end, running as if they were running for their lives. Some of the other cows, surprised by the commotion in the center aisle, began to swish their tails with nervousness, and a few others pulled back against their stanchions. Instead of the quiet sound of cows licking up the last of their feed, there was now the crashing, banging, jingling and jangling of the stanchions and the rat-a-tat-tat of hooves hurrying down the barn aisle.

I could hardly believe it. I had been so close to getting one of the heifers into a stanchion. And now all three of them were gone. The sudden disappointment made my arms feel as heavy as if a bag of barn lime was strapped to my wrists.

But what in the world had frightened the heifers?

Our cows got nervous once in a while if they saw something out of the ordinary in the barn, like our dog, Needles, suddenly coming around a corner when they didn't expect to see him. But Needles, a long-haired cream-colored Cocker Spaniel and Spitz mix, could not have scared the heifers because he was with Dad, picking corn. No matter what my father was doing—plowing, disking and planting crops in the spring—cutting and baling hay during the summer—or harvesting corn or soybeans in the fall—Needles went to the field with Dad so he could keep an eye on things.

The barn cats could not have frightened the heifers, either, because the heifers saw barn cats all the time, especially Tiger Paw Thompson, who liked to parade back and forth along the edge of the barnyard feed trough while the heifers were eating. The cat followed whoever was carrying feed to the barnyard, and then he would jump up on the feed trough. Sometimes the heifers licked him with their sandpapery tongues, and he would come away from the trough with sticky wet cow feed smeared all over his tiger-striped back.

But other than Needles or the barn cats, I could not think of anything that might have scared the heifers.

I put down the bucket and stepped over the gutter channel into the center aisle. To my left, on the other end of the barn, the three heifers were trying to go through the door all at the same time. I turned in the opposite direction—toward the door on the driveway side of the barn—and could hardly believe my eyes.

There, looking over the half-door, was my mother.

"What," I said, "are you doing out here?"

At the other end of the barn, I could hear the heifers, their hooves scrambling and scraping against the concrete.

"I...ah...well," Mom said, "I came to...well...to see if I could help."

As I turned my head to look at the heifers again, they finally discovered they had to go through the door one by one. The first heifer trotted outside, then the second heifer, then the third. And then I couldn't see them anymore.

"Boy," Mom said, "they're a little jumpy, aren't they."

Before I could answer my mother, our pickup truck pulled up by the gas barrel across the driveway from the barn.

"Dad's home!" I said.

My father opened the door and waited for Needles to hop out before getting out himself. Needles headed toward us, his feathery tail going in circles, as Dad rolled up the truck window and then carefully shut the door. Sometimes Dad slammed the pickup door. Sometimes he pushed it shut so that it closed with a quiet click.

"What are you doing out here?" Dad inquired.

I could tell my father was as surprised to see Mom in the barn as I was.

My mother moved one crutch to the side and slid her foot toward it so she could turn to face Dad.

"I thought maybe I could stand by the calf pen to keep those heifers from running up in front of the cows," she said.

Often when we were putting heifers into the stanchions for the first time, or if Dad had bought some new cows at an auction, they ran up in front of the mangers because they were afraid and didn't know where to go.

Beneath the bill of his blue-and-white chore cap, my father frowned and a puzzled look came into in his eyes. "What do you mean, keep them from running up in front of the cows? The heifers don't run up in front of the cows," he said.

Now it was my mother's turn to look puzzled. "But I thought...well...all I've been hearing for the past week is how much trouble you've had getting those heifers into the barn."

Dad took his cap off and slapped it against his leg. The top of his cap and the shoulders of his blue chambray work shirt were covered with a fine layer of dust kicked up by the corn picker. He put the cap back on his head.

"We've had trouble getting the heifers *into* the barn," my father said. "Once they forget about that feed trough outside, they usually go right into their stanchions."

My mother stared at Dad, her eyes as round as the two fifty-cent pieces I kept in a little wooden box on my dresser.

"You mean to tell me that all this time when you said you had trouble getting the heifers into the barn, you meant that you literally had trouble getting them *into* the barn? That you didn't have trouble getting them into the stanchions, but *into* the barn?" Mom said.

"That's right," Dad replied.

My mother started to laugh. "Ha-ha-ha, ha-ha!"

"What's so funny?" Dad inquired.

"You should have seen them," Mom gasped.

"Yeah, you should have seen 'em, Daddy!" I said. "I got them to come in the barn, but then Mom scared them, and they ran away. They all three tried to go through the door at once."

Dad grinned. "How long did it take 'em to figure out they had to go one at a time?"

I fingered the collar of my barn shirt, an old white blouse of my sister's that she said was too short to properly tuck into the waistband of her skirts. "I don't know. Maybe a minute. They kept pulling back, going forward and getting stuck and pulling back and going forward."

"Ha-ha-ha," Mom said as she wiped her eyes again. "I was a *big* help, wasn't I."

My father rubbed his ear. "You got out here just at the right time, I'd say. Or maybe it was the wrong time."

He turned to me. "I suppose we'd better see where those heifers went to. I hope they didn't end up at the back of the farm."

"At the back of farm?" I said.

Dad nodded. "You know how some of those Holsteins are. When they're riled up, there's no telling *where* they'll go."

"Hmmmmm," Mom said, "I guess you don't need me out here anymore. I'm going back to the house."

"We'll be in for supper after we get the heifers inside," Dad said.

My father opened the half-door, stepped into the barn and latched the door behind him. We walked down the center aisle together to the other door, and as soon as we came out of the barn, we saw the heifers.

They were not at the back of the farm.

They were waiting by the feed trough.

For the next forty-five minutes, Dad and I chased the heifers around the barnyard. Every time we got them close to the door, they stood for a few seconds, staring into the barn, and then they turned around and galloped away, tails held high in the air, kicking up their heels. After a while, the heifers must have gotten tired of the game—or else they were hungry—because eventually, all three of them trotted into the barn.

"Quick," Dad said. "You go in ahead of me, and then I'll shut the door behind us before the heifers can run outside again."

Once the heifers were in the barn, it only took a few minutes to get them into their stanchions.

"Tell you what," Dad said as we headed toward the house for supper. "If you want to put the cows in tomorrow, that's fine, because it *would* save time for me, but don't worry about the heifers. Leave them out in the barnyard, and then when I come home, we can get them in. And while you're waiting for me, you can ride Dusty. You might as well take advantage of this weather while we've got it."

Dad glanced at me and his right eye closed in a wink.

"Well," Mom said when we walked into the kitchen, "did you get those heifers in?"

"Finally," Dad said as he hung up his chore cap. "And here's what we're going to do after this. The kiddo is going to put the cows in, but she's going to leave the heifers out in the barnyard. And while she's waiting for me to come home so we can put the heifers in, she's going to ride Dusty."

"Ride Dusty?" Mom said.

"Yes," Dad replied. "She's going to ride Dusty. There's no sense in those heifers getting so riled up that it takes forty-five minutes to put them in the barn."

My father glanced at the clock, an old butter-yellow Time-A-Trol on the wall by the kitchen sink. "It's later now than if I'd put the cows in myself when I got home."

Mom sighed, and I noticed she had a funny expression on her face. If I didn't know better, I would have said she looked like she was ashamed of herself.

"Yes, it's later than normal. And that's my fault. I'm sorry," my mother said. "I should have realized when she said the heifers were hard to get in that there was something to it."

I could hardly believe my ears and turned to stare at my mother.

"I can tell you one thing, though," Dad said.

"What's that?" Mom asked.

"I'm never again making the mistake of feeding heifers outside, if I can help it."

For the rest of the week, I put the cows in after I came home from school, and then, while I waited for Dad, I would go out to the pasture to get Dusty.

On Saturday morning, Dad took the feed trough down, and once the feed trough was gone, within a few days, the heifers started coming into the barn with the cows and went into their stalls as if they had been doing it all along.

"Should have taken that trough down in the first place," Dad muttered when the heifers started coming in by themselves.

My father was right, I think. Old habits do die hard. Not necessarily as far as the heifers were concerned, however—but for Dusty. For the rest of the fall, whenever I helped Dad put the cows in and then walked out of the barn afterward, Dusty would be waiting by the fence between the barnyard and corncrib, nickering, her head bobbing up and down.

I never for a minute, though, fooled myself into thinking my pony wanted to go for a ride. No, what she *really* wanted is to get out in the yard so she could pick grass. During the four days that I rode Dusty after putting the cows in, I spent half my time pulling her head up, urging her a few steps forward, pulling her head up, urging her forward...

Oh, well—at least I had a chance to spend an hour with my pony on a few warm October afternoons when I got home from school. And that was a habit I could most definitely get used to.

****

~ 4 ~
# She'll Be Comin' Round the Cornfield...

A week ago the sky had clouded over and it had rained hard
throughout one entire night. Dad had stopped picking corn
for a couple of days to let the cornfield dry out. When he
started picking corn again, instead of warm and sunny as it had been
only a week ago, the weather had turned cold and sunny. Very cold. So
cold it was enough to make a person glad her mother had insisted she
put on a stocking cap and mittens. And a winter coat. And winter boots.
Even though the ground was bare and there was no snow anywhere.

My friends from school were also wearing stocking caps and
mittens and winter coats and boots. We were lined up along the back of
the corn wagon like those big stuffed animals in the booths at the
county fair that you could win if you threw a ball and knocked down
enough pins. The air was as clear and sparkling as the water in the
spring running next to the driveway, and the sun glinted like the gold
tooth that flashed in the smile of the man who worked at the feed mill
in town. Yellow cobs of corn came out of the corn picker chute above
the wagon and fell at our feet: *thud—thud—thud-thud—thud-thud-thud-
thud.* I turned toward the girl sitting next to me, and we both grinned.
My throat was already a little sore from yelling above the sound of the
tractor and the corn picker, but we were sitting close together, so we
could hear each other fairly well, at that.

"Hey! I know! Let's sing!" suggested one of the other girls.

"Yeah!"

"Let's sing!"

We looked back and forth at each other as more yellow cobs of corn
fell into the wagon—*thud—thud—thud-thud—thud.*

"But," one of my friends said, "*what* should we sing?"

Here in the wagon, with the bitter-cold wind behind us, the sun felt
warm on my face. During the summer, the wagon was used for loading
hay, but when fall arrived, Dad had attached the two-foot-high sides he
used to keep the corn from spilling onto the ground. The wagon was
painted red and so were the side pieces. The color reminded me of the
Macintosh apples we had bought on a Sunday afternoon trip to an
orchard not long ago.

I pulled my stocking cap down over my ears a little more as I considered what songs we could sing. I liked the one about "when Johnny comes marchin' home again," and then there was the one about the Camptown races and there was always *Twinkle Twinkle Little Star*...

"I know," said one of the girls. "Let's sing *She'll Be Comin' Round the Mountain*."

Just the other day we had sung *She'll Be Comin' Round the Mountain* in music class. Our music teacher at school pushed a piano from room to room, and when she came to our room each week, we often learned a new song.

"But—we're not going around any mountains!" another girl said.

Which was true enough. The cornfield—although not completely flat because it had a few small hills that Dad said were 'rolling' and that Mom called 'knolls'—was still one of the flattest fields on the farm. Dad had finished picking corn on our other place, a second farm my parents owned a mile away, and had now started picking corn in the field behind the big wooded hill we called the Bluff.

"How about..." one girl began, "She'll Be Comin' Round the..."

"...CORNFIELD!" shouted another girl.

"But what about the six white horses?" I asked.

"Well, let's see...instead of six white horses, we can sing 'she'll be drivin'...'"

Just then, Dad started to make another turn at the end of the cornfield.

"She'll be drivin'...THE RED TRACTOR!" we all shouted at the same time.

"What about the next part, though, about going out to greet her?" someone asked.

We all fell silent.

"I know," I said, "instead of singing about going out to greet her, we can sing, 'we'll all ride on the wagon when she comes.'"

"Yeah, let's do that!" someone said.

"But what about 'killing the red rooster?' Do we have to kill the red rooster?" asked another girl.

One verse of the song talked about 'killing the big, red rooster when she comes.' Mention of the word 'red' made me think of red apples.

"We can sing, 'we'll bob for red apples when she comes,'" I said.

"It might work out better" another girl said, "if we sing 'we'll bob for *bright* red apples when she comes.'"
We waited until Dad finished making the turn and corncobs were once again falling at our feet.
"Are you ready?" I asked. "Okay, let's start *now*—"
"She'll be comin' round the cornfield when she comes.
"She'll be comin' round the cornfield when she comes.
"She'll be comin' round the cornfield, she'll be comin' round the cornfield, she'll be comin' round the cornfield when she comes."
By the time we reached the last 'when she comes' I could hardly sing anymore. Every time I drew a breath to sing, a giggle bubbled up into my throat. My friends appeared to be having the same problem.
A while later, after the last giggle was gone, we were able to breathe again.
"She'll be drivin' the red tractor when she comes," one of my friends sang out.
We all joined in.
"She'll be drivin' the red tractor when she comes.
"She'll be drivin' the red tractor, she'll be drivin' the red tractor, she'll be drivin' the red tractor when she comes.
"Ohhhh, we'll all ride on the wagon when she comes. We'll all ride on the wagon when she comes. We will all ride on the wagon, we will all ride on the wagon, oh we'll all ride on the wagon when she comes.
"We will bob for bright red apples when she comes. We will bob for bright red apples when she comes. We will bob for bright red apples, we will bob for bright red apples, we will bob for bright red apples when she comes."
Once more, we had to wait for the giggles to go away. Then we started in again with—
"She'll be comin' round the cornfield when she comes.
"She'll be comin' round the cornfield when she comes.
"She'll be comin' round the cornfield, she'll be comin' round the cornfield, she'll be comin' round the cornfield when she comes."
For the past few minutes, I had noticed Dad glancing back at us with a tight-lipped expression. I often saw Dad press his lips together like that, usually when something happened that made him want laugh out loud, but he knew if he did, Mom would be upset. "Don't encourage her, Roy," Mom would say if she caught him smiling at me. Even though my mother was not out in the cornfield with us, I figured

Dad had gotten so much practice at not smiling, he had decided maybe he'd better not smile.

After a few more times of singing "She'll Be Comin' Round the Cornfield," the wagon was full—or as full as the wagon could get. A mound of corn in the middle sloped down to the two-foot-high red sides but only reached part of the way toward the back of the wagon where we were sitting.

At the end of the cornfield, Dad stopped the tractor, climbed down and walked past the corn picker. He paused at the front of the wagon and reached for an ear of corn, held the cob to his nose, and then, using both hands, snapped it in two. The corncob broke—*snick*.

Dad nodded and tossed the two halves back onto the mound.

"Sounds like you're having a good time," he said.

My father had pulled down the earflaps of his cap and had turned up the collar of his blue denim chore jacket. His face was red from the cold wind, and his blue eyes looked as blue as the sky.

"Can we ride on the wagon some more?" asked one girl.

"We have to take the load up to the corncrib and unload it," Dad said, "but after that, you can ride around on the next load, if you want to."

"Yayyyyy!!" I said.

"Thanks Mr. Ralph!" said one of the girls.

"I never knew picking corn was so much fun!" another girl said.

All along I had hoped that a Halloween party with my friends from school was going to be fun. I had never had a Halloween party before. A couple of weeks ago, I had asked if I could have one, although at first, my mother was not enthusiastic about the idea. Later on, after my big sister, Loretta, offered to drive my friends home on Saturday afternoon, Mom gave her permission for a party.

So, yesterday—the Friday before Halloween—four of my friends got on the bus with me after school. In the evening we bobbed for Macintosh apples in Mom's old, round, dented aluminum dishpan, played several games of Bingo and Old Maid, ate popcorn balls Loretta had helped me make Thursday night—and laughed until we almost made ourselves sick.

A couple of times, Mom told us not to laugh so much. "If you keep laughing like that, the next thing you know, you'll be crying," she said.

From the time I was a very little girl, Mom had told me not to laugh too much because it would be make me cry. So far, it hadn't happened, but that didn't stop Mom from telling me it *would*.

After a while, my big sister had intervened on our behalf. That's what my mother said when my sister, or my brother, or Dad thought maybe Mom should try not to be quite so strict—she said they were 'intervening on my behalf.'

"Mother," I had overheard Loretta say last night, "they're girls. And that's what they're going to do at a Halloween party is laugh."

My mother had sighed, and with a 'Heaven help me' look on her face had said, "Well, yes, I suppose you're right."

Today, after we had eaten breakfast—pancakes Dad had made when he came into the house after doing the morning milking, because pancakes were his specialty—we spent the rest of the morning playing with the calves and the cats, riding my pony, Dusty (with my big sister standing by to supervise to make sure no one got hurt, which was Mom's idea), and climbing the willow trees across the road from our driveway.

Climbing the willow trees seemed just dangerous enough to be fun. The willow trees grew at the edge of the marsh along the road, and if we weren't careful and fell out of the tree, we would land in the shallow pools of water standing among the bunches of brownish-yellow marsh grass.

When we grew tired of climbing the willow trees, dinner was nearly ready, and we discovered that Mom had made hamburgers and macaroni and cheese. After we had finished eating and had stacked our plates by the kitchen sink, one of the girls asked what we were going to do next.

And that's when I discovered the awful truth.

I had run out of ideas.

And we still had the rest of the afternoon before my sister was planning to take everyone home.

Dad was getting ready to go outside again and had finished zipping up his chore jacket and putting on his chore cap. With his hand on the doorknob, he had turned to us and said that if we wanted to, we could ride on the wagon while he picked corn.

For two whole loads, we rode up and down the cornfield behind the corn picker in the bright sunshine and the cold wind.

Lucky for us my father didn't mind listening to so many performances of "She'll Comin' Round the Cornfield."

Or maybe he did—because that was both the first and the last time I ever rode behind the corn picker, by myself *or* with friends.

****

~ 5 ~
Faster Than the Time Before

"Would you please go downstairs and get some potatoes for supper?" Mom said. I had already changed out of my school clothes, and when my mother spoke up, I was about to ask if I could have a piece of cake to fill the empty spot in my stomach so I would be able to make it until supper without starving to death.

While I stood there in the kitchen looking at my mother, a chill ran up my spine. Just the mention of the word 'downstairs' gave me chills.

Mom held out a small, square pan, the one we called the potato pan because long ago she had realized that it would hold enough potatoes to make the right amount for a meal.

I swallowed hard, hoping the butterflies which had suddenly appeared in my stomach would go away as quickly. I wasn't sure why the funny feeling in a person's stomach was called butterflies because butterflies were nice. I liked watching them come to the puddles in the driveway for water after a summer rain, dozens of yellow wings fluttering back and forth as they landed on the ground. The feeling in my stomach was more like piles of maggots twisting around, trying to find a way out. I had seen maggots on a calf that had died which Dad put by the pole shed until he had time to bury it. Hundreds of the small, white, slimy worms had made crackling, slithering noises as they crawled around on the dead calf.

"O-k-kay," I stammered, resisting the urge to clutch at my stomach. "I can g-g-get potatoes."

Mom looked at me sharply.

"Something wrong?" she asked.

"N-n-ooo," I said.

"Are you cold?"

I nodded and rubbed one hand over the goosebumps that had popped out on my arms.

"Are you getting sick?" she asked, frowning.

I shook my head. "No, I don't feel sick."

"Come here," Mom said.

I went over to my mother, who was sitting in her chair at the end of the table by the stove. Mom always sat by the stove, and Dad always sat on the opposite side of the table directly across from her. My mother's legs were not strong enough for her to run up and down the steps any time she felt like it. Because of the polio, if she wanted to go upstairs, or down to the basement, she had to crawl on her hands and knees. That's why it was my job to fetch potatoes from the basement for supper, although sometimes Dad would get potatoes when he came in the house for his afternoon coffee break.

My mother laid her hand against one side of my forehead, and then she moved her hand to the other side of my forehead.

"Hmmm…you don't feel like you have a fever," she said.

I knew how I felt when I had a fever: hot on the outside, as if I had been pulling weeds in the garden beneath the summer sun for many hours, but cold and shivery on the inside, the same way I felt when it was twenty degrees below zero and I had forgotten to put a sweater on underneath my chore coat before I went out to help Dad with the milking.

"No, Mom," I said. "I don't have a fever. I'm fine. And I'm not sneezing. Or coughing. Or anything."

"I guess maybe it is a little chilly in here," Mom said. "I let the fire go out in the woodstove this afternoon because I didn't think it was cold enough for a fire."

I was surprised my mother had let the fire go out. Mom often said she felt cold and that she figured it was because she couldn't move around as much as other people.

"Why don't you go upstairs and get a sweater," Mom said. "You'll feel even colder in the basement."

The basement stayed cool during the hottest of summer days, so at this time of year, it would be colder yet in the basement. I set the potato pan on the table and hurried upstairs to find a sweater. Better to let Mom think I was cold than for her to know the real reason for my chattering teeth. I knew if I told my mother that ghosts lived in our basement, she would never understand.

I was not alone in thinking our basement was haunted. Not necessarily our basement, I guess, but my friends from school were pretty sure their houses were haunted, too.

One girl said she stayed away from their back porch because she had heard scratching noises coming from inside of a box. Her mother had assured her it was just a mouse, but my friend thought it sounded awfully big to be *just* a mouse.

Another girl avoided an empty bedroom in their house. She had been walking past the room one day when the door slammed shut. Her father said the door had slammed shut in a cross draft from an open window, but my friend believed that any room with a door which closed by itself was a room to watch out for.

And another girl said she thought she had seen someone watching her through their living room window one evening. Her mother said it was only a shadow from the tree in the front yard, but my friend had decided she would not go into the living room after dark anymore unless the curtains were drawn.

As for our basement, nothing had ever jumped out and grabbed me when I was down there by myself, but the place was dark and damp and a little musty, and I knew about places that were dark and damp and musty. That's where ghosts lived. Or maybe I should say that's where one ghost had lived in a book I had read not long ago. So it seemed entirely possible to me that 'something' might be lurking under the shelves where Mom stored her canning.

Or maybe behind the potato bin.

Or what about on the other side of the pressure tank?

The pressure tank was a silver upright tank big enough for me to hide behind—and I knew it was big enough for me to hide behind because I had done that once when my sister came downstairs. I had jumped out at her and yelled 'boo!' and she had screamed so loudly that Dad heard her from outside where he was working on the water pump.

If the pressure tank was big enough for me to hide behind, then surely 'something else' could hide behind the pressure tank, and since that was the case, I was *never* going to hide behind the pressure tank ever again.

Mom said my Norwegian great-grandfather had built our house in the late 1800's. The basement was made out of sandstone blocks he had quarried from the hill behind our barn. The few small windows only let in a little bit of light, especially on cloudy days, like it was today, although later on, when winter arrived and the sun set shortly after

4:30, it would be even darker in the basement when I went to get potatoes.

A short while later with one of Loretta's old sweaters wrapped tightly around me, I picked up the potato pan and headed for the dim, dreary cellar.

At the top of the steps, I flipped on the overhead light. I glanced at the bulb and thought it looked awfully small and alone, way up there on the ceiling all by itself.

Then I looked down toward the bottom step where the dark basement waited beyond.

I carefully moved my foot off the first step and down to the second one.

What was that whistling sound?

I stood on the steps for a minute, listening.

Okay, just the wind.

Maybe.

I slowly went down the steps until I reached the basement doorway. If I could have convinced myself to step into the basement, turning on the light might have been easier. But no. Standing at the foot of the steps and reaching around the corner to find the switch seemed like a much better idea.

After what felt like a very long time, I finally found the light switch.

And then the basement wasn't dark anymore.

Well—not *as* dark. The basement was full of plenty of shadows and places where the light didn't reach.

I took a deep breath and, holding the aluminum pan to my chest, ran to the potato bin in the far corner.

And here came the next hard part. I had to lean down and grope in the bin to find the potatoes. And while I was scooping up the potatoes, that meant I would not be able to look behind me.

Using both hands, I threw potatoes into the pan—waiting—waiting—for the feel of an icy, ghostly hand to touch the back of my neck.

I picked up the pan of potatoes and spun around.

Nothing there of course.

Now I had to get back across the basement.

Running, I soon discovered, was much more difficult while carrying a full pan of potatoes.

Without pausing, I reached out and shut off the light—and then I ran up the steps, certain that if I looked behind me, I would see I was not alone.

"H-h-here's the potatoes," I panted, setting the pan on the counter.

"You must have run up the steps again," Mom commented. She was sitting by the table, both hands pushed into a dish of hamburger to mix in eggs, cracker crumbs and milk for making a meatloaf.

"I always run up the steps," I said. "I like to count the seconds to see if I can go faster than I did the last time."

I unbuttoned my sweater and hung it over a chair.

"Not cold anymore?" my mother asked.

"No. I'm not cold anymore," I said.

"Boy, I remember the times I would run up those steps when I was a little girl," Mom said. "Don't laugh—but I used to think there were ghosts in the basement."

I looked at her for several long moments.

"You used think there were ghosts in the basement?"

"And upstairs, too," Mom replied. "In the closet."

"In the closet?" I said.

The closet was a long narrow space which sloped from the middle of the room to the eaves in the back.

Come to think of it, the closet *was* dark. Not damp and musty like the basement. But dark.

And before I had gone downstairs, I had reached into that closet for a sweater.

"Of course," Mom said, "the basement was different then."

"It was?" I said.

"Not completely different, it was the same basement and the same steps, but there was no entryway above it like there is now. We didn't build onto the house until you were born."

"What was it like then?" I asked.

"The steps came out of the ground outside, so to me, the basement seemed like a big hole in the ground under the house. I suppose it wasn't surprising that I was afraid to go down there by myself."

Mom smiled and shook her head. "Even at that, wasn't I the silliest little kid you've ever heard of?"

"No," I said. "I don't think you were silly."

"Well," she said, "maybe not. But my mother sure thought so."

In spite of Mom's confession about thinking there were ghosts in the basement, too, when she was growing up, the next time I had to go downstairs by myself, I still broke out in goosebumps.

And thanks to my mother, for a long time after that, I could hardly bring myself to get anything out of the upstairs closet, either.

****

6

If It Rains, It Pours

Any minute now, Dad would be coming in from feeding the cows, and then we would eat supper. Outside the kitchen window, a narrow band of orange and pink and lilac along the western horizon was all that remained of the sun. The rest of the sky was the dark purple color of the purple-and-white striped petunias my big sister had planted around the light pole one summer.

"What do you suppose is taking Dad so long?" Mom asked.

My mother and I were sitting by the kitchen table waiting for Dad. Loretta had already rented an apartment in the city where she worked so she wouldn't have to drive back and forth on snowy, icy roads every day. My sister worked as an assistant bookkeeper for the electric company that supplied electricity to our farm and to many other areas of the county. We didn't have any snow on the ground yet, but Loretta said if she waited too long, she wouldn't be able to find a place to live for the winter. Ingman was working the 3-to-11 shift at the creamery this week, so he also would not be here for supper.

I had finished setting the table a little while ago, and the cups, plates, glasses, knives, forks and spoons were in their rightful places, carefully arranged on the cloth that covered the table. The table covering wasn't really a cloth, but something called oil cloth, which was easy to wipe off after we finished eating. The cloth was white with gold lines running back and forth and across it, and in the squares formed by the lines were yellow and orange flowers. My mother liked yellow. It was her favorite color.

I was about to say, "I don't know what's taking Dad so long," when we heard the creaking of the springs on the screen door. A minute later, after removing his barn boots and jacket in the porch, my father opened the kitchen door.

"Well," he said, as he closed the door behind him. "Guess what we've got in the barn."

I didn't have to think about it at all. There wasn't much that *could* be different except—

"We've got a new calf!" I exclaimed.

Dad shook his head.

"It's not a new calf?" I said.

My father turned to hang his cap on the newel post by the steps leading upstairs. Dad left his coat and black rubber chore boots in the porch, but the cap always came inside. He said he never knew when he might need his cap in a hurry, and that if it was on the newel post, he would know exactly where to find it.

Dad held up two calloused fingers slightly yellowed from the iodine soap he used to wash the cows' udders.

"We've got TWO new calves," he said.

"Two?" I said.

When I left for school that morning, I knew one of our Holsteins was close to having her baby, but the next closest one was still a couple of weeks away. Seeing as the days were shorter and winter was almost here, more cows were giving birth to their calves. Dad arranged the breeding schedule so most of the calves would be born in late fall and winter. That way, when summer arrived, the cows would not be milking as much and the morning and evening chores would not take as long, so Dad would have more time to fix machinery, to cultivate corn or soybeans, or to cut, rake and bale hay.

"Who else had a calf?" I asked. "The one down on the end?"

Dad shook his head again. "No. Nobody else. Just Chippy."

The cow we called Chippy was an even mixture of black and white, right down to her speckled nose. Dad said her nose looked like chocolate chip ice cream, which was his favorite kind. The cow's full name was Chocolate Chip.

I looked at Dad and frowned. "Nobody else had a calf? What are you talking about?"

"Twins," he announced with a twinkle in his blue eyes. "We have twins out in the barn."

For a second there, I thought I had heard him say twins.

Then I realized that *was* what he'd said.

"Chippy had TWINS?" I said.

As far back as I could remember, none of our cows had ever given birth to twins, and to be honest, I didn't even realize it was possible for cows to have twins.

"They're cutest little heifers you've ever seen," Dad said.

No wonder Dad was so happy. A long time ago I had learned boy calves aren't worth as much as girl calves, and that's why you don't keep the bulls. Last year the cows had given birth to mostly bull calves, except for two.

"Are they identical twins?" Mom asked.

"No," Dad replied. "They're not the same. They're...ahhh...whatcha-call-its."

"Fraternal twins," Mom said.

"What do they look like?" I asked.

"They're black and white. Like their momma. And one has a chocolate chip nose," Dad said, heading toward the bathroom to wash his face and hands.

My mother put her hands on either side of the chair and pushed herself to her feet. "It's like they say, I guess. 'If it rains, it pours.'"

"If it rains?" I said. "What does rain have to do with twin calves?"

"Nothing," Mom said. "It's just a saying. It means that sometimes in life, things can go one way for a long time, and then all of a sudden, you get more than you bargained for, or at least, more than you expected."

"Oh," I said. "You mean like now, when we only expected one calf but we got two?"

"That's right," she said. "Last year we had all bull calves, or mostly bull calves. And now this year, here we've got twin heifers."

"Can I go out to see—errr, I mean, *may* I go out to see them right now?"

If I asked to do something by saying 'can I,' Mom would reply, "of course you are *capable* of doing what you are asking, but the question is, do you have *permission*?" I was hoping that if I remembered to ask by saying 'may I' Mom would be more likely to say, 'yes.'

My mother frowned and brushed a lock of dark curly hair off her forehead. "No, of course you may not go out to see them right now. We're ready to eat supper, as soon as I put the food on the table and your father finishes washing up."

From the bathroom on the other side of the kitchen I heard the sound of splashing water as Dad rinsed his face.

"The calves will still be there when we're done eating, kiddo," Dad called out. "And besides, they aren't completely dried off yet. When we're ready to milk, they'll be on their feet, and then it will be more fun to see them."

In my opinion, it was always fun to see new calves, even if they weren't standing up yet, and in this case, with twins. But—if Mom and

Dad both said I had to wait until after supper—I knew I would have to wait until after supper.

A few minutes, later Dad returned from the bathroom, and we sat down to eat. Mom had made meatballs and mashed potatoes and acorn squash from our garden. Even though I was hungry, supper seemed like the longest meal ever.

"Don't gulp your food," Mom cautioned. "Slow down and chew. Otherwise you'll make yourself sick."

I lifted the fork to my mouth and chewed carefully. But after three mouthfuls, the next thing I knew, I was eating as fast as I had been before.

My mother shook her head and sighed.

When we had finished eating supper, I quickly stacked the plates and carried them to the sink. Moving the plates from the table to the sink was hard work for my mother because she had to hold onto a chair with one hand and that left only one hand free to carry the plates.

After the dishes were stacked, I went into the porch, put on my rubber barn boots and my barn jacket, stepped out into the frosty night air and headed across the yard. Dad had already left for the barn, but he wasn't very far ahead of me.

As soon as I opened the upper half of the barn door, I could see that Dad had moved the older calves to another pen on the other side of the barn and that he had put Chippy and her children into the calf pen on this end. The other calf pens were narrower, and I supposed that Dad wanted Chippy to have more room, seeing as she had two calves to take care of. From the milkhouse on the other side of the wall at the back of the calf pen, I could hear the clatter of buckets and the tinkling of milker inflations as Dad put the milkers together. I closed the door behind me and made sure the latch had clicked into place so the door wouldn't swing open again. After the crisp air outside, the warmth of the barn felt as welcoming as a fire in the living room woodstove.

I climbed the calf pen and sat on the top board, looking at Chippy and her calves. The babies were both lying down in the straw. One was watching me, her eyes opened wide with surprise to see the strange creature that had climbed up on the calf pen. The other calf was sleeping, her neck curled around, chin resting on her hind leg.

Dad had said the twin heifers were black and white like their mother. Chippy was pretty much half white and half black, but I could see one calf was a little more white and the other was a little more black.

I wanted a closer look at the babies, so I climbed down inside the calf pen. Chippy was used to seeing me climbing around the barn. She stood beside her calves, ears flicking back and forth as she turned her head to look at me.

The babies, however, weren't at all sure what was going on. The one that was awake ran around behind her mother, while the other one lifted her head and then scrambled to her feet, nearly falling down as her tiny hooves became tangled in the thick bed of straw.

"It's okay babies," I said.

After a while, since their mother was not afraid, the calves could not resist their curiosity. The one that had gone behind Chippy peeked out at me from beneath her mother's neck and then inched her way around her momma's front legs, and the other calf, who had untangled her legs from the straw, turned toward me. At the same time, the twins pointed their noses in my direction and sniffed the air, nostrils twitching.

I wanted to avoid scaring the babies again and decided it would be best if I stood still for a few minutes. As I watched the babies, who in turn were watching me, I noticed one heifer was actually 'black on white' and that the other was 'white on black.'

I took one step toward the babies, and then I heard the barn door open. Dad brought the milkers into the barn, set them in the middle of the aisle and came toward the calf pen. Instead of climbing over the boards, as I had done, he opened the gate and came into the pen that way.

"What do you think?" he asked. "Aren't they cute?"

The youngsters had grown used to me standing in the pen, but when Dad arrived it was too much for them. Both of the heifers ran around behind their mother. One peered out at us from beneath her mother's neck, the other one stood with her mother's tail draped over her ears.

Dad laughed. "They're getting around pretty good already, aren't they."

Up until the time Dad came through the gate, Chippy had been standing in the middle of the pen, chewing her cud. The cow moved forward and pushed her nose toward my father. He put his hand on Chippy's forehead and began to scratch the crest between her ears. The cow's rough tongue licked the sleeve of his chore coat—*scritch,*

scritch, scritch. The calves, feeling brave once again, although still unsure of the situation, inched their way out from behind their mother.

Dad gazed at the babies. "You know, I would have been happy to have just one of them. I've heard that usually twins are small, but these heifers are both a nice size. Not overly big. But not tiny either."

"You said they were black and white, like their momma," I said.

Dad turned to look at me. "They *are* black and white," he replied.

I pointed out how the two calves were different, that one was 'white on black' and that the other was 'black on white.'

My father stopped scratching Chippy's forehead and moved around to her flank to get a closer look at the calves.

"You're right!" he exclaimed. "I hadn't noticed."

He reached down to pet one of the heifers. The calf backed away from his hand and ran into her mother.

"Mooooo-oooo," said Chippy, soft and low her throat, the way cows do when they are talking to their babies.

"Maaaaa," the baby answered in return and shook her head, as if to rid herself of the feeling that Dad's hand had left on her ears.

My father lifted off his blue-and-white chore cap and settled it back on his head.

"So, what are we going to name 'em?" he asked.

Naming the cows and calves was important. We had to give them names, Dad said, because how would you know which one you were talking about if they didn't have names?

"It's gotta be something that's sort of alike, seeing as they're twins, but different enough so we can tell 'em apart," Dad added.

Tired of the visitors and hungry for more supper, one calf began to nurse on this side of Chippy while the other calf went around to the far side. As calves always do, they nudged their mother's udder—and none too gently at that—while their tails flapped up and down. Chippy lifted one hind foot and then must have remembered it was her babies nudging her and carefully put her foot down into the straw.

And in the blink of an eye, I thought of the most wonderful names for the calves.

"Rags and Patches!" I said.

"Hmmmm," Dad replied, nodding, "Rags and Patches. Those are good names."

He looked first at one calf and then walked around the back of the cow to see the other one.

"But," he said, "which is which?"

"Rags is the mostly black one," I said.

"How come?" he asked.

"Because the white spots are jagged around the edge like rags are jagged," I explained. "But the other one's black spots are smooth, so they look like patches."

"Good enough," Dad said.

The calves finished their snack and stood side-by-side, keeping an eye on us. The calf with the jagged white spots was a little closer. I bent toward her.

"Hi Rags!" I said.

The calf hesitated, then slowly, putting one foot down in the straw and then the other, moved toward me. Using two fingers, I stroked the soft sleek hair on her forehead.

I looked at the other calf.

"Come here, Patches!"

The white calf with the smooth black spots shook her head, and then she, too, came forward. I touched her chocolate chip nose. Patches stared at me, blinked, stuck out her tongue and licked my finger.

"Well," Dad said. "Look at that."

Before we left the calf pen, Rags and Patches had settled down in the straw for another nap.

My father smiled. "All babies are alike," he said. "Eat and sleep."

Several days later, Dad moved Chippy back to her stanchion, and for two nights while we were milking, the noise in the barn was deafening as Chippy called for her babies and the babies answered back. "This is just about the worst part of farming," Dad muttered. "I feel so bad for the mommas when I have to separate them from their babies." On the third day, everybody settled down, and the barn was quiet again.

Over the next few weeks, I spent many spare moments with Rags and Patches, petting their silky hair and brushing them with the brush I used for Dusty. Rags and Patches seemed to like the attention because they would practically knock me down in their eagerness to be the first one I brushed. Both calves had a perfect ringlet at the ends of their tails, too. Chippy also had that kind of tail. Dad called them curlicue tails. I liked the curls on the ends of their tails so much that I asked Mom if I could have a comb to take to the barn. Every evening I spent a few minutes wrapping the curls around my finger and smoothing the hair to make sure their curls stayed in perfect order.

The other thing I liked about Rags and Patches is that since they were the only two calves in the pen, I could carry the pails myself and didn't need anyone to help me.

And then, just when Rags and Patches had learned that they were better off drinking from their own pails, instead of both of them drinking from the same pail, it happened again.

Another cow gave birth to twin heifer calves.

I could hardly believe it. We'd never had any twin calves, and then in the space of a month, *two* sets of twin heifer calves had been born in our barn. We named the second pair Betsy and Barbie, and after they were separated from their mother, I had four calves in the same calf pen to pet and to brush. Feeding them was more difficult, but Dad helped me figure out a way to do it by myself: carry two pails and set them down in front of the manger, carry the next two pails and set them down in front of the manger, lift two pails into the manger and, in two shakes of a lamb's tail, lift the other two pails in the manger before any of the calves got ideas about tipping pails and spilling milk.

A few weeks later, when I had become very good at feeding Betsy and Barbie and Rags and Patches, Rose and Petunia arrived.

Several weeks after that came April and May.

"What is going on?" Dad said. "Four sets of twin heifer calves—*in one year?*"

"Well, I guess I did say, 'if it rains, it pours,'" Mom said when we told her about April and May.

"Yes," Dad said, "you did."

"What are we going to *do* with all of them?" Mom asked.

"Aren't we going to keep them?" I said.

"No," Dad said, "we can't keep them. We only need a few replacements."

As soon as I said, 'aren't we going to keep them,' I knew we couldn't. We never needed more than a couple of heifer calves to replace older milk cows when the heifers grew big enough to have calves of their own.

And all at once, I was struck by a thought that was so terrible, I felt as if something had hit me in the stomach.

"What about Rags and Patches?" I said. "We can't sell Rags and Patches."

My father shook his head. "No, we're not going to sell Rags and Patches. Their mother is a good milker, and I'm thinking they will be, too. Besides, Chippy would never forgive me if I sold her twin daughters."

"Chippy would be mad at you?" I said.

Dad nodded solemnly. "Yes. I think she would. And you would probably never forgive me, either."

"But what about the rest of them?" Mom asked.

"We'll keep them for a while," Dad said, "until they get somewhat bigger."

"Well," Mom said, "since we have so many, when you are ready to sell them, just make sure you know which ones are Rags and Patches."

"Oh," Dad said, "I don't think you have to worry that they'll get mixed up."

"Why not?" Mom asked.

Dad looked at me and grinned. "They're our first twins," he said. "And they've got curlicue tails, just like Chippy. We would know Rags and Patches anywhere, wouldn't we."

I grinned at Dad in return, and the feeling that something had hit me in the stomach disappeared as mysteriously as it had appeared.

Of *course* we would know Rags and Patches anywhere.

Who could ever forget a thing like that?

****

7

The Experiment

I stood back and looked at the door of the round, white, wooden granary. The granary was almost full of soybeans, but I knew Dad had put plywood in front of the door so that when the door was open, the soybeans wouldn't spill out. The question was—to get the soybeans, could I climb up on the staves and reach over the plywood—or would I have to climb over the plywood and go into the granary? But if I went into the granary, an even bigger question was—could I get out again?

Whether I ended up reaching into the granary or going over the plywood really didn't matter. My mother had told me to get some soybeans, so I knew I had to try.

The sky was the dull gray color of the cement floor in the milkhouse, and a raw, damp wind blew out of the south. I knew the wind was out of the south because it was coming from the direction of the church, and I knew the church was south of our farm. The little white granary stood next to the garage. The driveway circled past the house, the machine shed, the big granary, the barn, the little granary and the garage. In back of the round wooden granary was the large silver maple that shaded the gas barrel. The silver maple had long since dropped its leaves, and the bare branches rattled in the wind, sounding like teeth clicking together.

I pulled the collar of my coat closer around my neck. We didn't have any snow yet, but Dad said it might not be long until the ground was white.

I stepped forward and reached for the short piece of two-by-four that Dad had nailed to the granary so it formed a latch to hold the door shut. I turned the piece of wood until it was straight up and down, and then I grabbed the spike Dad had hammered into the door to act as handle. My father had built the granary during the summer a few years ago, and when he had finished putting up the boards and shingling the roof, I had helped him paint it white. All of our farm buildings were white: the house, the barn, the garage, the big granary, the corncribs.

Painting, as I had discovered, was not only easy, it was also fun. Dip the brush into the coffee can of paint Dad had gotten ready for me and then move the brush up and down and back and forth. Dip the brush into the paint again and move it up and down and back and forth. When we were finished, Dad said I had saved him a lot of work and that he wouldn't have completed the job nearly so fast without my help.

A sudden gust of wind blew around the garage and rattled the branches of the silver maple again. I hadn't come out here to think about how much fun it had been to paint the granary. With the saucepan Mom had given me in one hand, I pulled open the granary door with the other, grasped the doorframe and hauled myself up onto the first section. The bottom part of the round granary was like the front part of a silo where it had square openings, and from here, I could almost see over the plywood.

And then, just as I was about to pull myself up farther, I remembered what Dad said.

When my father had finished unloading soybeans a few weeks ago, he had told me I must never go into the round granary. "Now that the granary is full of soybeans, I don't want you climbing around in there. The soybeans might not hold you," he'd said.

"What do you mean?" I had asked.

"They're like quicksand. You could sink and be covered up and suffocate," Dad explained.

"What does that mean? Suffocate?"

"It means you can't breathe. And if you can't breathe, and you can't get out, you might die," he'd said.

Oh, great. I *would* have to remember what Dad said about the granary. Mom told me to get soybeans, but if I couldn't go right into the granary and if I couldn't reach them from the door, how was I going to get them? I knew Dad wouldn't say something like that about suffocating for the fun of it. He was always careful around the farm and made sure he shut off the tractor when he had to work on the hay baler or the corn picker or the combine, so the machinery wouldn't accidentally start up when he had his arms and hands inside.

I thought about my promise to Dad for a few moments, then I unzipped my coat and tucked the saucepan down the front. I grabbed hold of the doorframe with both hands and pulled myself up on the next stave. Now I could see over the top of the plywood. The little granary was almost full of soybeans.

I leaned over the plywood and stretched out my hand.

I…could…almost…touch…the…soybeans…and…maybe…if…I stretched…a bit farther…

But it was no good. I couldn't quite reach—

No, wait! Maybe I *could* reach the soybeans. The saucepan had a handle on it, and the length of the handle might be enough.

I pulled the saucepan out of my coat, grasped the end of the handle, and reached into the granary. The edge of the pan rested against the soybeans, and I discovered that if I wiggled the pan back and forth, soybeans would roll over the edge. If I kept doing this for long enough, maybe I would end up with enough soybeans.

As I lifted the nearly-full pan of soybeans out of the granary, I heard footsteps on the blacktop behind me.

"What are you doing up there?" Dad asked.

I turned to look at him.

"You weren't thinking about going into the granary, were you?" he asked.

I shook my head. "No, I wasn't going to go into the granary. I'm getting some soybeans," I said.

My father peered up at me from beneath his chore cap. "I can see you're getting soybeans. What I want to know is *why* are you getting soybeans."

I held the pan toward him. "Here," I said.

Dad took the pan from me. "Good crop of soybeans this year," he said, as he stirred the beans with one finger.

After a last look around from what I imagined it would be like to be a very tall person, I grabbed the doorframe and lowered myself onto the next stave.

"You still haven't told me what these are for, you know," Dad said.

"An experiment," I said.

"Oh, I see," Dad replied. "They're for school."

I stepped down to the ground and turned toward my father. "No, not for school. For Mom."

Dad stopped stirring the soybeans. "What?"

"They're for Mom. She wants to try an experiment. She's going to bake them."

I liked experiments. We did experiments in science class at school. Just the other day, we had taken dull, dark-brown pennies and had rubbed them with salt. The salt had turned the pennies bright and shiny again.

"Ma's going to do what?"

"Bake the soybeans. Like baked beans. Mom says soybeans are very nutritious."

Dad handed the pan back to me.

"She read all about it in the newspaper," I explained.

That's what my mother had said when she told me to get the soybeans—that she had read an article in the newspaper about how nutritious soybeans were and how you could bake them and make baked beans. "We've got a whole granary full, so I want to try it," she'd said. Mom made baked beans sometimes, but before this, she had used white beans she bought at the store. She said they were called Great Northern Beans.

"I know soybeans are nutritious," Dad said. "For cows, anyway. If we've got plenty, I like to mix them with the corn and oats when I go to the feed mill. Soybeans are high in protein."

About once a week, Dad would load up the pickup truck and go into town to the feed mill to make ground feed for the cows. During the summer, I went to the feed mill with Dad all the time, but after school started, I wasn't able to go to with him anymore.

"I suppose it *would* be interesting to see how the baked soybeans turn out," Dad said.

"I'm going to take these to the house," I said.

"And I've got to feed the cows," Dad said.

On my way back to the house, I studied the soybeans in the pan. They were round and light brown—like the color of the eggs we bought from a neighbor—and had tiny black dots on one end.

Each spring, Dad planted soybeans in one field or another, and many times when we were driving around with the pickup truck to check the crops, we stopped at the soybean field. Dad would eat a few of the beans to see how well they were ripening, and the first time I tasted raw soybeans, I was surprised to find they reminded me of peanuts. Dad said the reason soybeans tasted like peanuts was because peanuts and soybeans are both legumes. When I had asked what legumes were, he said legumes were plants that put nitrogen back into the soil. He didn't have to explain about nitrogen. I knew what nitrogen was—nitrogen was fertilizer.

When I walked into the kitchen, Mom asked me to put the pan in the sink.

"I'm going to wash the soybeans," she explained, "and then I'm going to boil them and let them sit overnight."

"When will they be ready to eat?" I asked.

"I'll bake them tomorrow. We'll have them for supper tomorrow night," Mom said.

I was pretty sure my mother would not let me stay home from school so I could watch the soybeans bake.

"But Mom, if you bake them tomorrow, I won't be here for the experiment!"

"Yes, you will," she said. "For the best part, anyway. Eating them."

The next afternoon as the school bus went up and down hills and around curves, I kept thinking about the soybeans and Mom's experiment. My mother's regular baked beans were sweet. She added plenty of molasses, brown sugar and some onion and bacon for flavor.

The school bus stopped at the end of our driveway, and I climbed down the steps and headed up the hill. I figured there wasn't much of a reason to hurry. The baked soybeans probably wouldn't be ready to eat until supper, anyway, although there was a slim chance they might be done and sitting in the oven to stay warm.

As soon as I opened the porch door, I could smell the soybeans. The scent grew stronger when I opened the kitchen door. The air was thick with the aroma of molasses and onion and bacon. That's how Dad described an odor, by saying the air was 'thick with it'—pine trees warmed by the sun, blackberries blossoming around the big wooded hill behind the barn, or gasoline that spilled over while he was filling the tractor.

Through the doorway connecting to the living room, I could see Mom sitting by the picture window, working on her embroidery.

I set my books on the table and went into the living room.

"Is your experiment done yet?" I asked.

Mom shook her head as she tied off a section of embroidery floss. "The beans will have to bake for a while longer, until supper."

Sometimes when Mom made baked beans, she would let me taste them even though they still were not quite finished baking. A small dish of baked beans with a bit of butter and some crumbled Saltine crackers on top sounded really good right about now.

"Can I taste them?" I asked.

My mother paused as she thought about my request. "No. I want them to be a surprise for all of us. If you're really hungry, and I suppose you are because you usually are when you come home from school, there's still some of those oatmeal cookies left."

After I had changed my clothes, eaten my cookies and had gone out to the pasture to pet Dusty, I went to the barn. The cows were already in their stanchions, and Dad was working on giving one or two more scoops of feed to the cows that milked the heaviest.

"Hi-ya kiddo," Dad said. "What's the news about the baked soybeans?"

"They're not done yet," I said.

"Well, then," Dad said, "I guess we'll just have to wait until suppertime to find out, won't we."

While my father went up to the haymow to throw down hay for the cows, I walked along in front of the stanchions with a broom to push in the feed that the cows had swept out of reach with their tongues.

By the time we finished feeding hay, my stomach was as empty as the bulk tank after the milk hauler pumped out the milk, and I thought it was possible I could eat the whole casserole of baked soybeans myself.

When Dad and I came into the kitchen, I saw right away that Mom had already set the casserole dish of baked beans in the middle of the table. I bent toward the dish to get a closer look, but the cover was still on, so I couldn't tell much.

Besides baked soybeans, Mom had made fried potatoes, fried ham (we'd ham for Sunday dinner) and green beans that we had grown in our garden last summer.

My mother waited until Dad and I were sitting at the table before taking the cover off the baked soybeans.

"Well," she said, reaching for a serving spoon that sat beside the casserole dish, "let's see how these turned out."

Mom dipped the spoon into the baked soybeans. She lifted the spoon and dipped it into the dish several times. Then she frowned.

"These beans *still* didn't absorb very much liquid," she said. "I thought they would. They've been baking all day."

Each time Mom dipped the spoon into the beans and lifted it, hot syrup made of molasses and brown sugar dripped off the spoon. Instead of stirring baked beans, it looked as if she were stirring soup.

I glanced at Dad, and he lifted one shoulder in a shrug.

"And look at those soybeans," she said.

I leaned forward. Regular baked beans turned brown, like the caramels wrapped in cellophane Dad bought at the grocery store. The soybeans were almost the same color as they were when I brought them in the house yesterday.

"That's what I thought would happen," Dad said. "Soybeans have a lot of oil in them, so I suppose that's why they didn't soak up as much molasses and brown sugar."

My mother looked at Dad, eyes narrowed. "Oil? How come you didn't say anything about oil before this?"

Dad shook his head. "You never asked."

My mother threw a withering look in Dad's direction, sat down and folded her hands. I folded my hands, too, and Dad bowed his head. "By thy goodness, all are fed, we thank the Lord for daily bread. Amen," Mom prayed.

My mother reached for the spoon and put a spoonful of soybeans on my plate. She waited for Dad to spoon some onto his plate and then put a spoonful on her own plate.

"Mmmmm," Dad said after he had tasted a forkful. "These are pretty good."

"Yeah, Mom. These are good," I said.

My mother finished chewing a forkful of beans. "They don't taste much like baked beans," she said, "but they do have kind of a nutty flavor."

"Like peanuts," I said.

"I can't figure it out, though," Mom said, stirring the beans on her plate with her fork.

"What's that?" Dad asked.

"The article in the newspaper said soybeans would bake just like regular beans and that you wouldn't be able to tell the difference."

Dad reached for the bowl of fried potatoes. "Maybe it depends upon the soybeans," he said.

"What about them?" Mom asked as she passed the bowl of green beans to me.

"This is the best crop of soybeans we've had in years," Dad said.

"Are you saying our soybeans are better than the ones they used to test the recipe for the newspaper?" Mom asked.

"I don't know if they're better," Dad said, "but maybe ours have more oil."

"How do you know they tested the recipe?" I asked.

"She's got a point," Dad replied. "They might've just figured all beans would be the same."

My mother wasn't quite smiling, but she looked happier than she did a few minutes ago. "I guess I never thought of that," she said.

In the end, my mother decided the experiment was a failure and that she wouldn't make baked soybeans again.

Personally, though, I didn't think Mom's experiment was a failure. After all, if my mother hadn't tried it, then I wouldn't have found out baked soybeans taste as good as they do fresh from the field.

And isn't that what experiments are all about? Learning something you didn't know before?

****

~ 8 ~
The Lesser of Two Evils

By the time I headed across the yard toward Dusty's pasture, the sun was already hanging low in the sky. I knew I would not be able to ride my pony before supper, but it was Friday, and Mom had said that according to the weather forecast, tomorrow was supposed to be a sunny day and that after I had finished helping with the cleaning, I could ride Dusty.

Every Saturday, my big sister, Loretta, cleaned the house from top to bottom. Mom, who couldn't do much of the heavy work because of the polio, dusted the downstairs bedroom and the living room, cleaned the bathroom and washed the floor. It was my job to dust the two upstairs bedrooms, shake all the rugs, sweep the porch, and wash the steps going upstairs from the kitchen. I would much rather be outside helping Dad—sweeping the barn floor or the machine shed floor, for instance—but Mom said it wasn't fair to expect Loretta to do all of the work. "You live in this house too," she told me.

When I had reminded Mom that Dad and Ingman also lived in the house, but *they* didn't do any cleaning, my mother had given me one of those looks which told me I was approaching dangerous territory. "As soon as you spend as much time as Dad does milking cows, putting in crops and fixing machinery, or as soon as you get a job at the creamery, like Ingman has, and you spend as much time as he does working around the farm, then you may be excused from cleaning," she'd said.

I still didn't like the idea of spending so much time every Saturday dusting, shaking rugs, sweeping the porch and washing the steps, but I also knew Mom had a point and that it would not be fair to expect Loretta to do all the work. Like it wasn't fair when a few of the girls in school—the ones who wore something brand new every week, a blouse or a skirt or shoes or socks—picked on a new girl in our class because her clothes weren't as nice as theirs and because she didn't eat hot lunch every day, but instead, always brought peanut butter sandwiches. The new girl was nice. She said she didn't mind eating peanut butter sandwiches and wearing hand-me-downs because it meant her little brother could get the medicine he needed.

At any rate, cleaning wouldn't take all day, and as Mom also mentioned, by afternoon, the sun would have a chance to take the chill out of the air.

With that happy thought, I arrived at the gate leading into Dusty's pasture. The little wooden gate was in the corner by one of the big silver maples my great-grandfather had planted around the edge of the yard. I couldn't see Dusty from here, so she was either below the hill, picking whatever grass she could find, or else she was standing by the old chicken coop on the other side of the granary.

We didn't have any chickens, and I could barely remember when we did have chickens, although what I could remember most was Mom saying she didn't like the chicken manure they left in the yard and Dad saying that because of where the chicken coop was situated, he couldn't build a pen for them. Mom had said it would be just as easy to buy eggs from a neighbor. And so, that had been the end of the chickens.

The chicken coop was still there, though, and after Dusty came to live here, Dad said she could use it for her own private barn. So far, Dusty hadn't used her barn very much. We had led her inside several times, but she always turned around and came right back out. When it was raining, she would stand with her head inside the door, but she wouldn't go all the way into the chicken coop. If Dusty wasn't below the hill picking grass, she would be standing on the other side of the granary, by her chicken coop. Going across the yard to the wooden gate put me halfway between the two places where I might find Dusty.

I reached for the latch, opened the gate, closed it behind me and latched it again. But even before I finished latching the gate, I knew Dusty was below the sidehill. I could hear her coming—*thud, thud, thuddity, thud*—as she galloped up the hill.

"Weeee-heee-heeee," said Dusty as she ran toward the gate.

When my pony heard the gate hinges creak, she often came on the run, hoping I had a carrot or an apple core or a piece of cookie for her. Dusty liked almost everything I liked to eat for a snack—except oranges and bananas. She wouldn't touch oranges and bananas.

I turned around to say 'hello' to Dusty…

…and for a split second, I wondered if someone had switched ponies on me.

Only this morning a thick white forelock had been growing from between her ears that was long enough to nearly cover her eyes.

But—where Dusty's forelock used to be—all I could see was a solid clump of cockleburs as big as the softball we played with at school.

Cockleburs, in my experience, were terrible things. They prickled and itched and stuck in your socks and got you in trouble with your mother when they stuck to your sweater. Especially sweaters like the one your sister had knitted for you out of light blue angora yarn that you weren't supposed to wear outside to play, but you did anyway, although you weren't really playing, you were on the way out to tell Dad something and got sidetracked. And then your mom had to use a razor blade to cut the cockleburs out of the sweater, and the sweater was never the same after that. Oh, yes—I was well acquainted with cockleburs.

I took a step toward my pony.

"Dusty," I said, "*what happened?*"

The pony nickered and trotted toward me. When we were only a few feet apart, she slowed to a walk and covered the last few steps, her head bobbing in time with her feet.

I reached out to pet her soft brown nose. Then I carefully poked the knotted forelock with one finger.

Cockleburs, I immediately noticed, which Dad said were also called burdocks, were as prickly when they were stuck in your pony's forelock as they were when they were stuck in your socks.

"How am I going to get those out?" I asked. "I don't think Mom will let me use a razor blade…"

My voice trailed off as I noticed that Dusty's mane was full of cockleburs, too.

And so was the feathery hair on the back of her legs.

But if I thought her forelock, mane and legs were bad—they were nothing compared to her tail.

I slowly walked around behind Dusty—and felt like sitting down right then and there to have a good cry.

What had once been long and white was such a solid mass of burrs, it looked like a club. Not a stick. Not a baseball bat. But a club.

"Hi, kiddo."

I had been so busy looking at Dusty's tail I didn't even hear Dad come through the gate.

"Hi, Dad," I said.

I walked around to Dusty's head. For some reason, I couldn't seem to take my eyes off her forelock.

"What are you doing out here, anyway?" I asked.

Dad came to stand beside me.

"I see you discovered where your pony went today," he said.

"Where my pony went?" I asked, although I knew she had gone somewhere because hardly any cocklebur plants grew in her pasture.

"What happened?" I asked.

My father sighed. "That little rascal snuck out on me while I was bringing the tractor through the gate by the corncrib."

Dusty was an expert at escaping through gates. One time when Dad was driving the manure spreader through the barnyard gate, Dusty had come at a dead gallop. I had jumped up and down and waved my arms, but the pony never even slowed down. As the manure spreader went through the gate, Dusty slipped through right next to it. There wasn't room for me to slip between the manure spreader and the gate, much less a pony, but somehow, Dusty made it through just fine. And then we had spent the next half an hour, chasing her around the barnyard before she would let us catch her.

"She went through the gate?" I said.

Dad reached up to rub his ear. "Couldn't stop her."

Dusty tried to swish her tail, but it was so heavy with cockleburs it did little more than bounce off the back of her legs.

"Boy, you wouldn't want her to slap you with that if she was trying to swish flies, would you," Dad said.

During the summer, if a vicious, blood-thirsty fly was biting her, Dusty would flap her tail up and down and then swish it from side to side hard enough that if she caught my bare arm or leg, it stung like the nettles growing along the barnyard fence. I didn't go out of my way to touch the nettles, but sometimes I couldn't help it when I was switching the gates around after milking so the cows would either stay closer to the barn or could go to the back pasture.

"But how did she get so covered with them?" I asked.

My father reached down to pick the burrs off Dusty's front legs. The feathery hair growing on the back of Dusty's legs was covered with burrs, but a few of the burrs were stuck to the front of her legs, too.

"When I tried to catch her, she thought it would be fun to go behind the corncrib," he said.

The narrow section behind the corncrib and the fence was filled with cocklebur plants almost as tall as me. All last summer, Dad kept saying the cockleburs looked really healthy and that he wished the corn in a few rocky spots in the cornfield looked that healthy. My father also kept saying he ought to cut them down with the scythe, but it was one of those little jobs he never quite got around to doing.

"When I went in there after her, she went out the other side," Dad continued. "If she'd only made one trip, it wouldn't have been so bad. But when I walked around the corncrib, she saw me and went back the other way again."

I could easily picture what had happened. Dusty was good at turning quickly and running in the opposite direction.

I tried to pull a few burrs out of Dusty's forelock. The burrs were so tightly twined in her hair that they wouldn't budge. All I got for my effort was a few pickers poking out of the end of my finger.

"That wasn't the worst of it, though," Dad said. "How many trips back and forth do you think she made before she finally let me catch her?"

If Dusty didn't want to be caught, she could play 'keep away' for a long time.

"Three?" I guessed.

Dad shook his head. "Try ten."

"TEN? Why didn't you get a bucket of feed?"

"I *did* get a bucket of feed. She still wouldn't let me catch her."

Cow feed was Dusty's favorite food in the whole world. Dad said we could only give her a handful at a time, otherwise she would eat until she made herself sick. When I said I didn't think ponies could throw up, Dad said not that kind of sick, but she could either develop a stomachache, which he said was also known as colic, or something called founder, which would make her feet hurt.

"I think it was like a game of 'Ring Around the Rosie' for her," Dad said. "She sure seemed to be having fun."

After trying to pick a few more burrs out of her forelock, I gave up.

"Don't worry about it now. It'll be dark soon, anyway," Dad said. "You can get them out tomorrow when you can see what you're doing."

The sun had already set, and the air was starting to feel much colder.

"Okay, Daddy," I said.

The next day, as the weather forecast had predicted, the sun was shining out of a bright blue sky. I finished shaking the rugs and dusting upstairs and washing the steps, and then I headed out to Dusty's pasture.

"We're *supposed* to be going for a ride, you know," I said, as I pulled Mom's scissors out of my back pocket. Mom said I could use her scissors as long as I carried it to the pasture in my pocket and brought it back in my pocket. "I don't want you tripping over something and stabbing yourself," is what my mother had said.

I put the scissors to the knot of cockleburs between Dusty's ears, worked the point of the blade into the knot and made a careful snip. Not much happened, except Dusty realized she had found the perfect opportunity to rub her forehead against my ribs.

"Hold still," I said.

I worked the blade into the knot again, and this time, a small lump of cocklebur and forelock fell to the ground.

Bit by bit, I shaved off the burrs. Dusty must have thought it felt good to have the burrs cut out from between her ears because as I worked, she stood still and didn't try to rub her forehead on my ribs again.

When I was finished, little clumps of burrs and white forelock littered the ground at our feet, scattered among the dry, brown leaves from the silver maples. I was so used to seeing the pony with a thatch of white hair almost covering her eyes that I couldn't help myself and nearly laughed out loud. All of the burrs were gone—and so was every strand of Dusty's forelock. She reminded me of the men I saw in town who wore crew cuts.

Now that the forelock was out of the way, I could concentrate on Dusty's mane. As I looked at the tangled mess, I wondered if it would be possible to pull the burrs out instead of cutting them out. Maybe the burrs weren't stuck as tightly in her mane as they has been in her forelock.

I took a small section of mane between my fingers and tugged at the burrs. But nothing happened. The burrs were there to stay.

I pushed my fingers through the handle of the scissors—and drew in a sharp breath as the metal pressed against the back of my hand. When I was finished with the entire job (and at the rate I was going, it would take hours), my fingers would probably be black-and-blue.

Minutes later, the first clump of mane hair dropped to the ground. I grabbed another section of mane and set to work, wincing when the handle of the scissors dug into my fingers.

Although Dusty had been standing quietly for a long time, suddenly, she threw her head up and nickered. I turned to see what Dusty was nickering at.

"Need help?" Dad asked, as he let himself through the gate.

"Hah! Don't you look funny, Dusty," he said.

Another strand of mane dropped to the ground. I pulled my hand out of the scissors and wiggled my fingers.

"Hand getting sore?" Dad asked.

"My fingers hurt, and now I'm getting a cramp in my thumb," I said.

Dad put his hand in his pocket and pulled out his pocket knife.

"Let's see how this works," he said.

Dad always kept his pocket knife sharp. He often used it to cut twine strings on hay bales, but once or twice, I had seen him use it to shave a little wood off a door so the door would close better, and one time, too, he had used it to cut off a piece of Dusty's hoof that had broken and was sticking up at a funny angle.

My father grabbed a handful of mane, sawed at it with his pocket knife, and in no time at all, the tangled lump dropped to the ground.

"Tell you what," Dad said. "I don't want you to use the knife because it's sharp. And if you cut yourself, Ma will have my hide. But if you could hold up the mane while I cut, it'll go a lot faster."

I looked at Dad. "Mom said I shouldn't ask you to help me because you've got lots of other work to do."

My father shrugged. "You didn't ask me. I asked *you* if you wanted my help. Besides, this is all my fault."

Ever since the time Dusty had slipped through the gate while Dad drove the tractor and I stood there jumping up and down and waving my arms, I knew it was nobody's fault but Dusty's when she got out.

"That wasn't your fault, Daddy," I said.

"Well, no, maybe not," he said. He scowled at the brown pony with the light brown dapples. "It's *your* fault, Dusty. I don't know why you think it's so much fun to escape through gates."

A long time later, when I was beginning to think we would never finish, Dad shaved the last of the cockleburs out of Dusty's tail.

I stood back to look at the pony—and felt a lump rising in my throat.

Dusty's mane and tail, although thick and somewhat bushy, had been so pretty. But instead of a long, white tail that nearly brushed the ground when she walked, almost half the length was gone and what was left reminded me of the bristly scrub brush I used to wash the steps. Along her neck, spiky, uneven patches of short white mane waved back and forth when she put her head down to graze. The only part of her mane that had not been cut off was a handful by her withers. Dad said we should leave a handful of mane so I would have something to grab onto if I needed it when I was riding my pony.

"Oh, my goodness, Dusty," said a voice from behind us.

I turned around. It was my big sister.

"You've been out here so long, I wanted to see how you're doing," she explained as she let herself through the gate.

Loretta was wearing her usual Saturday outfit for cleaning: a pair of faded black pedal pushers, an old blouse and white tennis shoes. She walked all the way around Dusty, and as she completed the circuit, I noticed she was biting her lips.

"You can laugh if you want to," I said.

Loretta shook her head. "No, I'm not going to laugh. It's just that, well—she looks—well—she looks *different* without her hair."

Dad took a couple of steps back so he could see the pony better.

"Could've been a lot worse, I suppose," he said.

I looked at Dusty with her stubby tail, spiky mane and missing forelock. "Worse?" I said, turning to stare at Dad. "How could it have been *worse*?"

"Barb wire," Dad said. "Don't you remember? I keep my rolls of barb wire behind the corncrib. The whole time Dusty was running around back there, I was so afraid she would step in that wire."

I was all too familiar with barb wire. No matter how careful I was, I would sometimes tear my pants and scratch my leg while crawling through a barb wire fence. The cuts were never deep, but a barb wire cut felt like a row of bee stings along my skin and was sore for a few days until it started to heal. One of our cows had gotten her leg wrapped up in some barb wire, too, a few years ago. The cow's leg was swollen, and she was limping. Dad had spent a long time washing out the cuts and scrapes and dabbing on iodine. The cuts finally healed, but the cow's leg had been covered with scars from her knee down to her foot. One cut on my leg from the long barbs hurt bad enough, so I could very well imagine how the cow had felt.

"Yes," Loretta said. "It *could* have been a lot worse. Dusty's legs might have been cut to pieces. Looks like it was the lesser of two evils, if you ask me."

"And her mane and tail and forelock *will* grow back, you know," Dad said.

'The lesser of two evils' was one of Mom's favorite sayings. Sometimes Mom would tell me I could take my pick between two chores, such as helping Loretta wash the outside of the windows—or washing the windows on the inside. "You can decide for yourself which is the lesser of two evils," she'd say.

To tell you the truth, neither one sounded like much fun. When I helped wash the outside of the windows, Mom would stand on the inside and point out all the spots I had missed, even though I wasn't finished yet. When I washed the inside of the windows, Mom would stand behind me and point out all of the spots I had missed, even though I wasn't finished yet. A few weeks ago when Mom had asked me which one I wanted to do, I had decided I would rather wash the outside of the windows, even though it meant washing the same window four times before Mom was satisfied. At least if I washed the outside of the windows, I could be *outside* on a beautiful fall day.

"Say," Loretta said, "I thought you were going to ride your pony this afternoon."

"I was," I said.

"You still can," Dad replied. "For a little while, anyway."

Most of the afternoon was gone, but I didn't have to set the table for supper yet, and a few minutes later, I led Dusty toward the granary so I could use the step by the granary door to get on. I hopped on Dusty's back and rode around to the gate where the pony had escaped.

From here I could see behind the granary—and behind the corncrib next to it.

"You went through *there*, Dusty?" I said, although I knew she had because many of the brown, bristly cocklebur plants were knocked flat.

And in among the cockleburs were six rolls of barb wire. After Dad replaced a fence, he kept the used wire because he said he never knew when he might need some extra.

No wonder Dad was worried my pony would get tangled up in the barb wire.

"What's the lesser of two evils, Dusty?" I said. "Cuts all over your legs—or a haircut?"

But I didn't even have to think about that one. If Dusty had become tangled in the barb wire, instead of cutting burrs out of her mane and tail and forelock, I might have spent my time this afternoon washing out cuts and scrapes and dabbing on iodine.

If it was up to me, I'd take the haircut any day.

And so would Dusty, I'm sure.

∗∗∗∗∗∗∗∗∗∗∗∗∗∗∗∗∗∗∗∗∗∗∗∗∗∗∗∗

~ 9 ~
The Mysterious Red Coat

Only one piece of clothing remained in the closet. I lifted the hanger off the bar and struggled to hold up the weight of the heavy coat. The red wool coat had been hanging in the closet in the small hallway between the kitchen and the bathroom for as long as I could remember. Mom and Dad's bedroom—which my mother said used to be the living room before they built onto the house—was on the opposite side of the hallway.

I could not picture Mom and Dad's bedroom as a living room. But then, I also could not picture the house with only two rooms downstairs (a kitchen and a living room). My mother said my great-grandfather had built our house as a temporary place to live. He had started to build a much larger house, she said, but in the fall, a forest fire had burned it down, and with winter coming, they needed shelter. As it turned out, he never did get around to building another house.

I pulled the coat out of the closet and turned toward my mother.

"You can leave that where it is," Mom said. "Nobody will be wearing it."

During all the years the coat had been in the closet, I had never seen anyone wearing it, and in fact, the only time I saw it out of the closet was when my mother cleaned.

Every spring and fall, my mother cleaned the closet and rearranged the summer and winter clothing so it was easier to find what she and Dad needed. Since the polio made it difficult for my mother to get in and out of the closet, part of my job involved removing the clothes and putting them on the bed.

I turned the hanger holding the red wool coat so I could get a good look at the back of it. Then I hung the coat in the closet again, seeing as my mother had I should leave it there.

"Mom? What's that coat for?"

My mother paused in wiping off shoe boxes. She was sitting on a chair in the hallway next to a pail of water with pine cleaner in it. When my mother cleaned, she sat on a chair to do the work. Her legs were not strong enough to hold her up for very long.

"What do you mean, what's it for?" Mom replied. "It's a coat."

"I know that," I said. "But I've never seen anybody wear it. It's Dad's isn't it?"

"Yes, it is."

"So how come Dad has a red coat?" I asked.

The most colorful thing I had ever seen my father wear was the red bandanna handkerchief he kept in the pocket of the blue denim overalls he wore when he worked around the farm. Dad did not always carry a red handkerchief, though. Sometimes he carried a blue one. And when he carried a blue handkerchief, he was dressed all in blue: pants, blue chambray work shirt, denim chore jacket, blue-and-white pin-striped cap.

Mom leaned forward to pull out more of the boxes that I had moved toward the front where she could reach them. "That's a hunting coat," she said, her voice sounding muffled.

I was almost certain my mother had said 'hunting coat,' but since she was leaning forward, with her head inside the closet, she must have said something else that only sounded like hunting coat. Maybe she'd said—'morning coat' or 'evening coat' or 'special coat.'

"What did you say?" I asked.

"I said," Mom replied, pulling back out of the closet, "it's a hunting coat."

"A *hunting* coat?" I said.

"Yes, a hunting coat."

I stared at her in astonishment. "Like for deer hunting?"

She nodded.

"But Dad doesn't hunt!"

"Not now," she said.

"Not *now*? You mean he used to?"

Mom pulled another box out of the closet. "He did a long time ago. Before you were born. Would you go out in the kitchen and get another scrub pail ready? While I'm wiping off boxes, you can be wiping down the walls inside the closet and scrubbing the floor."

Ever since I was big enough to help with the cleaning, or rather, from the time I was old enough to know what my mother meant when she said things like, 'wipe down the walls, not like that, use the whole cloth and go up and down and back and forth—and be sure you dip the rag in the pail and wring it out for each new section you're washing,' it had been my job to wipe down the inside of the closet. Mom said it was easier for me to get in the closet than it was for my big sister, seeing as she was taller than me.

I had taken two steps toward the kitchen when Mom cleared her throat.

"No, wait," she said. "I guess I wasn't thinking, was I. If you're going to wash the walls, you might as well put that red coat on the bed with everything else."

I pulled the red coat out of the closet, laid it on the bed, and then I went to the kitchen.

I stood at the kitchen sink, filled a pail with water and thought about Dad going hunting. My father said animals have feelings like we have feelings and that they deserve to live their lives the way we deserve to live ours. Could it really be possible that he had gone hunting? He also did not like guns, and as far as I knew, he had never owned one. The fathers of some of my school friends went deer hunting, though, and after Thanksgiving, some of the other kids talked about eating venison.

I had never tasted venison, and one time when I had mentioned that a few of the kids at school had been talking about venison for supper, Dad said I hadn't missed much. "It's gamy," he said, "bitter-tasting, from all the acorns the deer eat."

I turned off the faucet and carried the pail of warm water and Pinesol to the closet and stepped inside. At least wiping down the closet on the inside wasn't as bad as cleaning the little storage space under the steps that we called the pantry. The smell of pine cleaner became almost over-powering in the pantry.

Half an hour later, when I was finishing up the closet floor, my father came in for his afternoon coffee break.

"Daddy, I never knew you went hunting," I said, as I dumped the pail of dirty water down the drain in the kitchen sink.

Dad poured a cup of coffee for himself and then reached into the cookie canister for a handful of cookies. We usually had cookies in the cookie canister. My sister liked to bake cookies, and her favorites were chocolate chip, oatmeal and sugar cookies.

"Went hunting with Reuben and Gar," Dad replied. He sat down by the table with his cup of coffee and cookies.

Reuben and Garfield were my mother's cousins. Mom was an only child. Reuben and Garfield were older than Mom, but they had grown up not far away and used to help my grandfather with his farm work.

Dad and Garfield often went fishing together. Sometimes Reuben went
with them. I had never heard of anyone else named Garfield. His first
name was Jens and his middle name was Garfield, Mom said, but he
preferred being called Garfield. Sometimes Dad and Gar would let me
go fishing with them. Garfield would bait my hook for me, like Dad
would, and then he would tell me where to cast my line, also like Dad.
     "Where did you go hunting with Reuben and Gar?" I asked.
     "Oh," Dad said, "we went someplace up north."
     'Up north' covered a big area. On several occasions we had gone
picking blueberries 'up north,' and the trip took a long time, a couple of
hours in the car. But Dad said there was much more 'up north' north of
that yet.
     "When you went hunting, how come you wore that red coat and not
orange?" I asked.
     Dad dipped a cookie into his coffee. "That's what everybody wore,"
he said. "They didn't have orange hunting clothes back then."
     "Why don't you go hunting anymore?"
     Dad finished chewing his bite of cookie and swallowed. "I only
went once," he said.
     "Once? You never went again?"
     Dad shook his head. "Nope. Just that one time. I didn't really want
to go, but they talked me into it."
     He took a sip of coffee and reached for another cookie.
     I pulled out a chair and sat down by the table.
     "But Dad, it looks like a very nice coat."
     My mother stood by the sink, rinsing out the scrub pail. "It *is* a nice
coat. Heavy. And it's made out of good wool, too."
     I snitched a cookie off Dad's pile. "Just because you're not going to
wear it for hunting, you could still wear it. It's a really pretty color."
     My mother sat down at the other end of the table. "That's right,
Roy. You could still wear it. Kind of a shame to have that nice, heavy
wool coat but not get any use out of it."
     Dad picked up his coffee cup and looked at me and then at Mom.
"Yes, it's a nice coat. Maybe I will wear it."
     He took a sip of coffee and set the cup down on the table. "Of
course, you could wear it, too," he said to Mom.
     "Me?" my mother asked, looking startled. "Why would I want to
wear it?"
     "Why not?" Dad said.

"But *where* would I wear it?" Mom asked.

"When we go to town?" Dad replied.

"Hah!" Mom said. "Can't you see me wearing that bright red coat to the grocery store? People stare at me enough as it is right now."

Whenever I went anywhere with my mother, I saw people staring at her. Not everyone, of course. Not the people who knew her. But people who did not know her would stare as she made her way along, moving one crutch forward and swinging her leg out from the hip, moving the other crutch forward and then swinging her other leg out from the hip.

"Not *everyone* stares at you," I said.

"No," Mom agreed. "Not everyone."

"But they might if she was wearing that bright red coat," Dad said.

My mother turned a hard-eyed stare in his direction, saw that he was teasing and shook her head. "Oh—*you*!" she said.

For weeks after that, I waited to see if my father would wear the red wool coat. But he did not. Not even to the barn.

Actually, I guess I wasn't surprised. I think I always knew red just wasn't Dad's color.

Not that much red, anyway.

****

~ 10 ~
Chance Of A Lifetime

I reached for the blanket and pulled it up closer to my face. Ever since we had finished eating supper, I felt as if I would never be warm again. And I was sneezing. The tickle would start far up inside my nose, and then before I knew it—*AH-chooooo!* A little while ago when Dad was getting ready to go out to the barn, Mom had told me to rest on the davenport rather than go out to help my father with the evening milking.

"That's a good idea, kiddo," Dad had said as he zipped up his chore coat. "I can carry the milk and feed the calves by myself. I would rather do that than have you come outside in the cold when you're sick."

I was pretty sure Dad could do the chores all by himself. It would just take him a little longer without someone to carry the milk to the milkhouse and to feed the calves and to help feed hay and bed the cows down for the evening.

Thanksgiving was a few weeks away, and while it was not as cold as it would be in January, Dad was right—it wasn't very warm outside. When I had looked at the thermometer by the kitchen window after supper, the thin red line was only as high as the mid-twenties.

Thinking about the temperature outside made me shiver, and I wondered if I should get up to find another blanket. Except that finding another blanket would require going upstairs to the trunk where we kept the extra blankets.

"Are you still feeling cold?" my mother called out from the kitchen. She was in the middle of washing the supper dishes.

"A little," I said.

"Give me a minute to dry my hands, and then I'll come in and put some more wood in the stove," she replied.

The woodstove stood across the living room from the davenport, only a few feet away.

I sat up, fluffed my pillow, blew my nose and tossed the tissue into the paper grocery bag where there was already a small pile of used tissues. A couple of minutes later, my mother made her way into living room, grasping the arm of the davenport for support and then reaching for the chair next to the woodstove. The heavy iron door clattered when she lifted the latch and pulled it open. I heard *thunk...thunk...thunk* as she tossed sticks of wood into the stove.

I had no idea why they were called sticks of wood. Sticks were small, like Popsicle sticks or twigs from the maple trees around the yard after a windy summer thunderstorm. The wood that went into the stove seemed more like logs to me.

"There," Mom said, closing the door and latching it. "Once that wood starts burning, it'll warm up in here."

My mother returned to the kitchen. The clatter of the dishes as she washed them and the sound of the crackling fire in the woodstove were comforting, and soon I drifted off to sleep.

I don't know how long I had been asleep, but suddenly, it was as if someone had grabbed my hands and yanked me into a sitting position. Something—a sound of some sort—had awakened me. A sound that sounded like—

"Yeeeeek!" my mother shrieked. "Eek, eek, eek!"

Each of the 'eeks' was accompanied by a dull thumping sound.

I threw back the blanket and struggled to my feet. With my heart pounding, I followed the strange noises through the kitchen to the doorway of the small hallway beyond where I stopped and rubbed my eyes.

My mother was head and shoulders into the closet, taking aim with the broom, although she couldn't get in a good whack because of all the coats, clothes, shoes, boots and assorted boxes.

"What's the matter, Mom?"

My mother pulled back from the closet. One lock of her normally tidy curly dark brown hair had fallen across her forehead.

"Mouse," she gasped. "I was wiping the table when it ran across the kitchen and went into the closet."

"A mouse?" I said. "What kind of mouse?"

We had several different kinds of mice around the farm. There were the little gray ones. And the darker gray ones with big ears. And then there were the brown-and-white field mice...

"What kind of mouse?" my mother replied. "Well, let's see, it was—"

She stopped abruptly and shook her head. "I don't *care* what kind of mouse it was. What I *do* care about is that it's probably thinking of making a nest. In *my* closet."

My mother took a firmer hold on the broom and went back into the closet.

"All right you little bug—well, what I mean is, you little…you little…*mouse* you. Where are you?" my mother asked.

Mom, I knew, was about to say 'bugger' but then thought better of it. She said it was one of those words I wasn't supposed to use, but I wasn't sure why.

My mother kept bumping the broom against boxes and shoes and boots. Faint scrabbling and scratching noises came from deep within the closet. But no mouse appeared.

Mom came out of the closet and closed the sliding door. She reached up, pushed the lock of hair back where it belonged and looked over at me.

"Get a cat," she said.

"What?"

"Get a cat."

"A cat?"

"Yes, a cat. That's why your father says we have so many—to catch mice. So go out to the barn and get a cat."

I could hardly believe my ears. Mom wanted me to get a cat.

My mother liked to grumble about the number of cats around our place. When she went outside, several cats usually were sitting on the porch steps. Sometimes it was many more than several. Six, maybe. As my mother came out of the house, she would use her crutches to nudge the cats out of the way.

Most of our barn cats were tame, and the ones that liked to sit on the porch steps were especially tame. They were not alarmed by being nudged with a crutch. They would stand up, stretch and then leisurely walk a few steps and sit down to groom. This annoyed my mother because it meant the cats were still in her way.

"Shooo-shooo," she'd say. "Psssst! Move!"

The kitties would look at her, blink, stand up slowly and then saunter down the steps, where they would sit down again to groom. Which meant that after my mother had descended the porch steps, the cats were still in her way.

Getting down the porch steps, Mom said, often took longer than it did for her to walk to the car, and more than once, I had her declare that cats were 'useless creatures.'

"All they seem to do is sit around, get in the way, have kittens and drink milk," my mother would mutter under her breath.

Whenever Dad heard Mom grumbling about the cats, he would point out he hadn't seen a mouse in the granary or in the barn for a long time. "They catch rats, too," he said.

Mom continued to grumble about the cats. "They say you can tell whether the people who live in a house are kind or not by the number of cats you have to push out of the way to get to the front door. We must be just about the kindest people on earth," she would say whenever an especially large number of cats clustered on the porch steps.

But—after seeing a mouse run into the closet—Mom actually wanted me to get a cat! *And* bring it into the house!

For the time being, I forgot about not feeling very well. I went out to the porch and put on my barn coat and barn boots. The coat and boots were cold from sitting in the unheated porch, and I shivered as I zipped up my jacket. I grabbed my red stocking cap from its hook and jammed it on my head, and then I headed out into the dark, starry night. Across the yard, the barn lights glowed yellow through the windows, and I could hear the chuffing-wheezing sound of the milker pump. From the tracks a mile away came the rumble of train cars and the sound of the whistle as the engineer signaled at the crossing.

I went past the little pump house and past the corner of the garage, and the closer I got to the barn, the happier I felt. *Finally* we were going to be able to show Mom how useful cats could be. I knew just the one I wanted, too. The best mouser of them all—Tiger Paw Thompson.

While it was true that Tiger Paw Thompson loved to sit on the calf pen and pat the heads, faces and shoulders of anyone who came within his reach, he had turned into an expert mouser as well. Dad said he had seen Tiger Paw hunting mice in the haymow and in the granary. And one time I had watched him waiting patiently on the floor beside the feed box. Only the tip of his tail twitched, and even when a mouse stuck his head out from between the feed box and the wall, Tiger Paw did not move. He waited until the mouse came out from the shelter of the feed box, and then, faster than I could blink, he pounced and that was it.

Normally I would have felt bad for the mouse, but Dad said that mouse droppings in the feed might make the cows and calves sick.

'Oh, boy,' I thought gleefully as I reached for the handle on the barn
door, 'Mom won't grumble about the cats after *this*.'

Just then the barn door started to open. Dad was on his way out to
the milkhouse with a bucket of milk. My father did not scare easily, and
in fact, the only time I had seen him somewhat close to appearing
shook up was when I had run to the house, screaming, after seeing a
bull snake by the granary. The look on his face was as close to
unnerved as I had ever seen it.

"You shouldn't sneak up on people like that," he said.

"Sorry, Daddy."

Dad closed the barn door and headed to the milkhouse, the handle of
a full milker bucket clutched in his right hand, his left arm held out
from his body to help balance the heavy weight on the opposite side.

"You're sick. What are you doing here?" he asked as he reached for
the handle on the milkhouse door.

"I need a cat," I said.

Dad climbed the steps he had built to make it easier to dump milk in
the bulk tank

"A cat?" he asked, glancing at me as he began to pour the milk.

"Yes, a cat. There's a mouse in the closet, and Mom said I should
get a cat. I want Tiger Paw."

Dad smiled. "He was by the cat dish when I left the barn."

"I can hardly wait," I said. "Now we can show Mom why it's good
to have cats."

"Yes, I suppose it *would* be the chance of a lifetime, wouldn't it,"
Dad agreed.

I headed back into the barn, and sure enough, Tiger Paw Thompson
was sitting by the cat dish. The dish the cats drank milk from was an
old stainless steel frying pan which had lost its handle, and Tiger Paw
Thompson sat next to it, washing his face and his ears. When I picked
him up, surprised once again by how heavy he was getting, the cat
snuggled down in my arms and started to purr.

"Come on Tiger Paw. Let's show Mom that cats can be useful," I
said.

As I walked back to the house, Tiger Paw Thompson kept right on
purring. He was used to being picked up and carried around.

What Tiger Paw Thompson was not used to, however, was coming
into the house. None of our barn cats were used to being in the house.
As soon as I opened the door and entered the porch, the brown tabby

cat stopped purring. And when we reached the kitchen, he began to struggle.

In all the times I had picked up Tiger Paw Thompson and carried him around, he had never wanted to get down as badly as he did now. I could feel the cat's hind claws digging into the front of my chore coat, and I was quite sure that if I had not been wearing a coat, his claws would have dug through my shirt and into my skin.

"It's okay Tiger Paw," I said, stroking the striped head. "Mom wants you to catch a mouse. You like catching mice."

While I held the struggling cat, my mother opened the closet door, picked up the broom and began nudging aside boots and shoes and boxes. Like before, we heard scrabbling and scratches noises.

But no mouse appeared.

"Put the cat in the closet," she said.

I considered telling her that since Tiger Paw wasn't especially thrilled about being in the house, he probably would not want anything to do with the closet, either.

"*Put the cat in the closet,*" my mother repeated, a steely look coming into her blue eyes.

I put the cat in the closet.

In one frantic leap, Tiger Paw jumped out of the closet and made a beeline for the door. His tailed was fluffed to twice its normal size and he was meowing pitifully. It didn't take much to figure out that he was pleading with me to open the door for him.

So—I let him outside.

The last I saw of Tiger Paw Thompson for the evening, he was headed toward the barn, running as fast as he could go.

When I came back in the kitchen, my mother was still standing by the closet, holding the broom

"Hmmphhhh!" she sniffed. "I might have known. What good does it do to have cats if they won't catch mice?"

Dad came in from the barn a while later. I had returned to the living room and was huddled under the blanket. I sat up and pulled my knees to my chin so Dad would have a place to sit down.

"What happened with Tiger Paw Thompson?" my father asked.

Mom was working on an embroidery project. She pushed the needle into the fabric, and when she looked at Dad, I could see the steely expression had returned to her eyes.

"What happened?" she asked. "Absolutely nothing. That silly cat wouldn't even *attempt* to look for the mouse."

"He was really scared and wanted to go back outside right away," I explained.

"Oh," Dad said.

"I might have known," Mom added. "What good are cats if they won't catch mice?"

"The cats catch lots of mice," Dad said. "What can you expect? Tiger Paw Thompson isn't used to being in the house."

"Hmmpphhh!" Mom replied.

My father glanced at me and his right eye closed in a brief wink.

"It's like you riding a workhorse to go and get the mail," Dad said.

Every now and again, Mom and Dad talked about 'the good old days' so I knew that in the 'good old days,' the mail box was not at the bottom of the driveway, it was far away, far enough away so that sometimes people rode horses to get the mail. I had always thought it sounded like tremendous fun, riding a horse to get the mail

Mom looked at Dad, dark eyebrows raised high on her forehead.

"Me? *Me* ride a horse to get the mail? You've got to be kidding. I never did any such a thing. I was too afraid of horses to ride one to get the mail," she said.

I could see Dad was trying not to smile.

"Right," he said. "Just like Tiger Paw Thompson was afraid of being in the house."

"Hmmphhh," Mom said, although I could tell from the way she said it Dad had gotten his point across.

But that didn't change what had happened.

Poor Tiger Paw Thompson. And poor me, too. We had missed our one and only chance to show Mom why cats were useful to keep around.

Then again, maybe Tiger Paw had done some good, at that.

For the rest of the winter, Mom never did see or hear another mouse in the closet.

****

~ 11 ~
Pilgrims' Progress

Thanksgiving was only a couple of weeks away, and we were studying the Pilgrims in school. We read stories about the Pilgrims. We made bulletin boards about the Pilgrims. We colored pictures of Pilgrims. We completed worksheets about Pilgrims. We took tests on the Pilgrims.

And now we were supposed to do a project on the Pilgrims. Our teacher said we could make a display or paint a picture or write a story or do a report.

Before this, I had only thought of Thanksgiving as a holiday in the fall when I could eat as much lefse as I wanted. Ever since I was a very little girl, I had loved lefse—a paper-thin potato pastry (pronounced 'lef-suh') my mother said had been brought to this country by Norwegian immigrants. My grandmother and grandfather had both come from Norway, and Mom made lefse to serve along with the rest of Thanksgiving dinner. I would have happily eaten nothing else but lefse spread with butter and sprinkled with sugar and cinnamon, all rolled up into a log—if my mother would let me. Mom baked a couple of batches of lefse before Thanksgiving, and then between Thanksgiving and Christmas, she made some more.

Thanksgiving also meant two whole extra days off from school. After spending every day from August until November (except for the weekends, of course) working on arithmetic, penmanship, social studies and reading, I was ready for a vacation, and all together, between the lefse and two days of vacation, I could hardly wait for Thanksgiving. But up until now, I never realized we had Thanksgiving *because* of the Pilgrims. In school we had learned that during the Pilgrims' first winter they were in danger of starving and freezing to death but their second year was much better so that's why they invented Thanksgiving.

For the rest of the day after our teacher gave out the assignment, I thought about the Pilgrim project we were supposed to do, but it wasn't until the bus ride home that I remembered Ken and Barbie.

And once I remembered Ken and Barbie, I knew what I could make for a display.

Now all I had to do was convince Mom and Dad to help me.

And since I needed help from both of them, if I waited until supper, then I would only have to explain it once. Besides, tonight I would have them all to myself because it would only be the three of us. Ingman was working at the creamery, and Loretta was staying at her apartment in the city where she worked.

Later on, after Dad came in from the barn and I had set the table and Mom had dished up the food and we had said our table prayer, I put my left hand in my lap, crossed my fingers, and turned toward my father.

"Daddy? Do you have any wood I could use? Something flat that I could set things on?"

Dad paused in buttering a slice of bread. "Wood? What do you need a piece of wood for?"

"School," I said.

"Why do you need wood for school?" Mom asked.

"Because we have to do a project about the Pilgrims, and I want to make something," I said.

Dad finished buttering his slice of bread. "I've got a two-foot-square piece of plywood you can have. It's kind of an odd size for anything I might want to do with it. Will that work?"

"Thanks, Daddy!"

I turned toward my mother.

"Mom? Could you make some Pilgrim clothes for my Ken and Barbie dolls?"

I'd only had the Ken doll since the previous Christmas. I'd had Barbie for a while before that. I didn't play with dolls very often. I had a dog and a pony and the barn cats and the calves. Why would I want to play with dolls? But since I had both of them, why not put them to good use? That's what Mom said when something had been sitting around that she didn't use very often, and then when she found a use for it, she would say she was 'putting it to good use.' Old bedspreads, blankets, dresses and work overalls she tore into rags and sewed into strips for rag rugs also were things she 'put to good use.'

My mother set her fork down on her plate.

"Make doll clothes?" she replied. "But I was going to start making lefse."

"Please Mom?" I pleaded. "Couldn't you make the doll clothes *and* make lefse?"

My mother tapped her fingers against the table while she thought about it.

"I suppose I could sew a few doll clothes first," she said. "If you don't want anything too complicated."

I shook my head. "No. Nothing complicated. Just a dress for Barbie. And a shawl. And pants and a coat for Ken. And maybe one or two other things."

"A dress *and* a shawl. *And* pants *and* a coat for Ken? It's starting to sound complicated already."

"But Mom, it's for school."

"Well...all right. I guess I can make some doll clothes," she said.

I decided to wait until later to ask about the other items I wanted to borrow. I was afraid that if I asked now, Mom might say no.

After we had finished eating supper, while Dad was drinking his cup of coffee, I helped my mother clear the table. Dad usually waited until the table had been cleared, and then we went out to the barn together to start the evening milking. Tonight, instead of going to the barn, we went to the machine shed.

The day had been warm and sunny with a temperature in the fifties, but the night air was chilly, although it wasn't downright cold. It was the time of year, Dad said, when the weather didn't know if it should be fall or if it should be winter, and that's why it was cold some days and warm other days.

When we arrived at the machine shed, a long building across the lawn from the house that looked like a culvert which had been cut in half, Dad turned on the overhead lights. The bright red combine my father used to pick oats and soybeans was parked along the back wall. Ahead of that were the plow, the cultivator, the disc and the hay mower. The 460 Farmall was next. And in front of the four-sixty—or behind it, depending on how you wanted to look at it—was our pickup truck. My father put pieces of machinery in the shed in the order that he would need them. He drove the pickup almost every day, so the truck was closest to the door. He would need the four-sixty this winter to move snow and sometimes to haul manure when there was too much snow for the little Super C Farmall. He wouldn't need the plow and disc until spring. He wouldn't need the cultivator and hay mower until summer. And he wouldn't need the combine until late in the summer when the oats was ripe.

The small bulbs suspended from the arched ceiling gave off a dim light that left most of the shed in shadows.

"Should I get a flashlight, Daddy?" I asked.

"No," Dad replied. "I can see well enough to find what I'm looking for."

I watched as my father rummaged among the pieces of plywood leaning against the wall near the room he had built for the chest freezer.

"Here's the piece I was talking about. Will it do?" he asked.

The plywood was as Dad had described it: a small piece about two feet square.

"It's perfect, Daddy," I said.

He turned and carried the wood to the workbench along the opposite wall. "Here's some sandpaper if you want it," he said, setting the sandpaper on the workbench. Then he reached for his trouble light, plugged it in and hung it up over the workbench. "You'll need the trouble light to really be able to see what you're doing," he explained.

Dad turned to look at me. "First milker should be ready in about a half hour. Have you got your watch on?"

I pulled back the sleeve of my coat to show him my watch. The watch had a medium-sized face and a blue leather band. It was an Alice-in-Wonderland watch and had come with a ceramic figurine of Alice-in-Wonderland, who had long, blond hair and was wearing a blue dress, a white apron and black slippers. Alice stayed on top of my chest of drawers. I wore the watch every day. Loretta had given me the watch and Alice as a birthday present.

"Good. You've got your watch," Dad said. "That way you'll be able to tell when I need you to carry milk. I know how easy it is to get busy on a project and lose track of time."

He lifted his cap and settled it back on his head again. "You *do* remember the rule about my tools, don't you?"

I drew a deep breath and let it out quickly. "Of *course* I remember the rule. Put everything away where I found it."

My father never minded if I used his tools as long as I put them back where they belonged so he could find things when he needed them.

Dad nodded as he turned to leave. "That's right. Put everything back where you found it."

I stood for a few minutes, looking at the workbench and thinking about what I should do first. A little while later, when the milker pump started, I had picked up the sandpaper and was sanding the piece of plywood. I had watched my sister varnish the window sills in the living room, and before she varnished the sills, she had sanded them. The window sills had been smooth when Loretta finished sanding them, and I wanted the plywood to be that smooth, too.

After awhile, I glanced out the open shed door and was surprised to see Dad carrying a bucket toward the milkhouse. A half hour couldn't have gone by already, could it? I looked at my watch. Sure enough, a half an hour had gone by already. I put the sandpaper down, turned off the trouble light and the overhead lights and headed for the barn.

Over the next week, I went to the machine shed right after school and worked until supper, sawing, sandpapering, and carefully braiding pieces of twine string together. Sometimes I worked in the evening, too, before it was time to help Dad with the milking.

Finally, one afternoon I was ready for the clothes my mother had finished making only the day before.

"I hope these are all right," Mom said, as she held up the dress and the shawl.

My mother had drawn patterns on white paper, had cut out the black cloth and had sewn everything together by hand, because, as she had said one evening when I came in from the barn, "These bits and pieces are too small for the sewing machine."

Mom had made a brand new pair of black pants and a black coat for Ken. She had even crocheted a little black hat for him. The coat was more like a pullover shirt, but she had sewn buttons down the front. And Barbie had a brand new dress, a black dress with a full skirt and long sleeves, and also a brand new white crocheted apron.

My mother had also crocheted square white collars for both Ken and Barbie, seeing as the Pilgrims wore white collars. The shawl and collars and apron had been crocheted out of the same kind of white thread Mom used to make doilies and to edge pillow cases.

Before I dressed Ken and Barbie in their new clothes, I went upstairs to open the trunk sitting against the wall, and in the bottom corner, I found what I was looking for. Slowly and carefully, I made my way down the steep, narrow steps. I was used to the steps, but if I slipped and slid all the way to bottom and broke what I was carrying, I knew my mother would never forgive me.

I managed to make it to the bottom of the steps with everything in one piece.

"Mom, could I use this?"

I stood in the living room doorway and held up a tiny porcelain tray with two tea cups, saucers, and a miniature tea pot on it. The rim of each piece was decorated with gold paint.

My mother looked up from the magazine she was reading.

"Why on earth," she asked, "do you need my doll's tea set? It's very old. If anything gets broken—"

"It's for my Pilgrim display," I said.

"I kind of figured that. But if it gets broken, I can't replace it, you know. I've had it for, well, let's see." Mom stopped and frowned. "I've had it for, oh, more than forty years, I suppose."

"But Mom," I said. "It's for school."

My mother shifted in her chair and used both hands to pick up one leg so she could cross it over the other. My mother's legs were not strong enough for her to cross them the way another person would. Then she pulled off her black-rimmed reading glasses.

"I don't know if I like the idea of you taking my tea set to school," she said.

"I'll be careful with it," I said.

"What will happen if you don't take the tea set?" she asked.

I thought about that for a few moments. "Nothing will happen, but my display won't look as good without it," I said.

"How are you going to carry it all the way to school?" she asked.

I had already been thinking about how I would take everything to school.

"I'm going to wrap the tea set in newspaper, and then I'm going to put Ken and Barbie and the tea set into a grocery bag," I said.

"But what about after it gets to school?" she asked.

I had thought about that, too.

"You can send a note with me to my teacher telling her about the tea set so she can tell everyone why they shouldn't touch it," I said.

My mother folded her glasses and sat looking down at them as she thought about what I had said.

"Do you promise," she said at last, "to be very, very, very careful?"

"I promise," I said. "I promise I will be very, very, *very* careful."

"Okay, you may use my tea set," Mom said

I put the tea set on the table and began the task of dressing Ken and Barbie in their new outfits. When I had put the white collars on both of them and had set the hat on Ken's head, suddenly, they didn't look like Ken and Barbie anymore. They looked like the Pilgrims in the pictures we had colored in school. My mother had come out to the kitchen, and I held them up so she could see them.

"Say, they look pretty good, don't they," Mom said.

I left Ken and Barbie on the kitchen table, went out to the machine shed to get the rest of the display and brought it back to the house so I could see how it would look when it was set up.

The plywood had become a Pilgrim's kitchen, complete with a table and two benches. I had used twigs from the silver maple growing near the machine shed to make the top of the table. I had cut the twigs into shorter pieces, and I had tied them together with baler twine I had taken out of the twine barrel in the barn. When we opened bales of hay, we put the twine strings in a fifty-five gallon drum my brother had brought home from the creamery. I found out that if I pulled at the twine string long enough, it would separate into smaller strands, and that's what I used to tie the twigs together. I couldn't find any twigs that would work for the legs, so I had taken four of Dad's spikes and pushed them into the spaces between the twigs. The spikes, all shiny and silver, looked out of place with the table, but it was the best I could do. I had also used twigs to make benches for Ken and Barbie, except instead of spikes, the benches were held up by shorter nails.

To make the fireplace, I had gathered stones from along the driveway and had glued them together. The fireplace was really only a back wall an inch high with a fire ring in front of it made of stones, like the fire rings Dad and I made when we went fishing at the Norton Slough during the summer after milking. We always gathered stones so my father could build a smoky fire to chase away the mosquitoes. The stones in the Pilgrim kitchen looked about as much like a fireplace as Dusty looked like the horses that ran in the Kentucky Derby that I had seen on television, but it was enough to give the *idea* of a fireplace.

The rug on Ken and Barbie's floor also was made from twine string I had braided together and then coiled around in a circle to form a rug.

I put Ken on one bench and Barbie on the other. It took me a few minutes to bend them into position so they would sit on the benches.

Ken and Barbie both had flexible legs that bent at the knees. When Ken and Barbie were seated, I carefully picked up the tea set and put it on the table between the two of them. The table was kind of bumpy, I noticed, but as long as nothing jiggled the display, I thought it would be all right.

"Look, Mom!" I said.

My mother stood by the stove, with her back to me, stirring a pan of gravy. "Let me finish this and turn off the stove so I don't have to worry about it," she said.

A minute later, Mom switched off the burner and put the pan of gravy on a hotpad on the counter. She turned and reached for the nearest kitchen chair and made her way to her own chair. Moving from the stove to the table took all of her concentration, and she could not look at my display until she was sitting down. My mother carefully lowered herself onto the chair, and when she was seated, she shifted her attention toward my project.

"So *that's* what you've been working on all this time," she said.

As I was telling my mother how I had made the table and the benches, Dad came in from the barn.

"Look at that!" he said. "You're all done with your Pilgrims."

My father hung his cap on the newel post and came closer to the table.

"Benches, a table, a fireplace," he said, "and two Pilgrims who are about to have tea, it looks like. I'm glad I saved that piece of plywood."

"It turned out to be just the right size, didn't it," Mom said.

"How are you going to get it to school, though?" Dad asked.

"Oh, she's already got that all planned out," Mom said.

"I'm going to wrap the tea set in newspaper, and then I'm going to put Ken and Barbie and the tea set and the benches and the table into a paper grocery bag. I can put the handles over my arm, and then I can carry the other part," I said.

And that's exactly what I did.

The next day, I headed down the driveway even before we saw the bus coming on the main road. Most days I waited to leave the house until I saw the bus, and that gave me time to reach the bottom of the driveway before the bus arrived. Because our farm was situated on a hill, we could see the bus on the highway from the living room window before it turned onto our road.

I slowly walked down the driveway and stopped every once in a while to get a better grip on the plywood. I had to be careful because I wasn't sure if the fireplace would stay where it belonged, and I did not want to have to rebuild the fireplace. When I had almost reached the end of the driveway, the bus pulled up.

Climbing the steps of the bus with a paper bag over one arm and both hands occupied with holding the Pilgrims' kitchen was a little like trying to hop on Dusty's back while holding an ice cream cone, which I had done one time last summer. I almost made it, too. I was nearly settled on her back when Dusty took a step forward. I made a wild grab for her mane—and the ice cream cone ended up in the grass at her feet. Not that Dusty minded. My pony sniffed the ice cream cone, licked at it with her smooth tongue—and then, *crunch*—my ice cream cone was history. Dad said he didn't know ponies liked ice cream cones, but then he said he always knew Dusty was a different sort of horse all together, anyway.

Fortunately, I made it up the bus steps without any problems, and when I was safely in my seat, with the Pilgrims' kitchen on my lap and the paper bag between my feet, I breathed a quiet sigh of relief.

Forty-five minutes later after I arrived safely in my classroom, I breathed another quiet sigh of relief. I gave my teacher Mom's note about the tea set, and she told me I could set up my display on the counter near the window.

"Did you make that all by yourself?" my teacher asked, as I unwrapped the tea set.

"Yes," I said, "all except for Ken and Barbie's clothes. My mom made those. And my dad gave me the wood. And he let me use his tools. And his workbench."

"I see," she said. "Well, it's really quite...well...it's...ahhh...it's quite...inventive."

"What does that mean?" I asked.

"It means," she said, "that you used your imagination. I never would have thought of using spikes for table legs."

Some of my classmates had drawn pictures of Pilgrims. And some of them had written stories. A couple of kids wrote reports. Four of my classmates had gotten permission from the teacher to act out a skit they had made up about the Pilgrims. And three other kids had worked together to paint a portrait of a Pilgrim (one of them had stretched out on the floor on a long piece of paper, the kind of paper we used in art class that came on a big roll, and then the other two kids had traced the outline of his body).

But no one else had built a display.

Later in the afternoon as I got off the school bus, I could hardly wait to tell Mom that my teacher liked my project. The weather had turned cold again, and when I hurried up the hill, a strong wind stung my cheeks and brought tears to my eyes. I was glad my Pilgrim project was finished so I wouldn't have to spend time in the chilly machine shed this afternoon.

Two-thirds of the way up the driveway, I climbed the bank, cut across the lawn, rushed through the porch, and never even stopped to wipe my feet before opening the kitchen door.

"Guess what, Mom! Guess—"

"What?" Mom asked as she reached for the pancake turner.

I closed the door and set my books on the table. I was so eager to tell Mom about my Pilgrims that I hadn't even noticed the aroma of potatoes and flour and butter when I came into the porch.

"You're making lefse!" I exclaimed.

My mother transferred the piece of lefse from the griddle to the dishtowel sitting on the cupboard.

"I realized it was high time," she said. "Thanksgiving is next week."

Mom folded a white flour-sack dishtowel around the lefse. "Did you get to school all right? And did your teacher like the Pilgrim display?" she asked.

I told her about the bus ride to school and that no one else had built a display.

"And my teacher said it was inventive and that inventive means I used my imagination!" I said.

"Yes," my mother said, "I know what the word 'inventive' means."

A little while later I sat by the table with two pieces of warm lefse spread with butter and sprinkled with sugar and cinnamon. The Pilgrim display was finished. Mom was making lefse. And Thanksgiving was next week.

Life couldn't get much better than this.

What more could I possibly want?
Except maybe for another piece of lefse...

****

Great Expectations

Loretta poured a cup of coffee while she waited for the toaster to finish toasting two slices of bread. Because it was the Friday after Thanksgiving, my big sister had the day off from working at the electric company.

Ka-thunk! went the toaster as the lever popped up. The slices of toast jumped out of their slots and settled back down again. Dad said the toaster must have a good set of strong springs. Sometimes the toast jumped all the way out of the toaster.

"Are we going shopping today?" Mom asked

Loretta put the two slices of toast on a plate and opened the drawer to find a butter knife. "I *would* like to go today, but…"

"But what?" Mom replied.

"But—the stores are always so crowded the day after Thanksgiving," my big sister said. "It's hard to get any shopping done."

"Maybe we could go tomorrow," Mom suggested.

My mother said 'we' when she was talking about going shopping with Loretta, but the polio paralysis and walking with crutches made it difficult for her to get into the stores. Most of the time, she sat in the car while my sister shopped, although once in a while, she would venture into a store.

"That's what I was thinking," Loretta said, "that maybe tomorrow would be better."

She finished spreading strawberry jam on her toast and sat down by the table.

"I'm glad I don't have to worry about that today," Dad said as he reached for a box of Cornflakes.

"Worry about what?" my mother asked.

"Shopping," Dad said.

"You?" Mom said. "Shopping? You never go shopping. Not this kind of shopping."

"That's what I mean," my father said as he poured milk over his cereal. "That's why I don't have to worry about it today. Or tomorrow. Or any other day, for that matter."

"So," Loretta said, turning her head in my direction, "what would you like for Christmas this year?"

There it was. The 'big question' I had been waiting for—the question that I didn't have to think about.

"Ice skates," I said.

For several years, I had wanted a pair of ice skates. I wasn't exactly sure why I wanted ice skates. We didn't have a pond on our dairy farm. And no one in my family ice skated. Sometimes Dad said he skated when it was icy and he had go out to the barn, but he wasn't actually wearing skates, and it was only his way of making a joke to say it was slippery. Other than that, I had not heard anyone in my family talk about skating.

I had read stories about ice skating, though. *Hans Brinker and the Silver Skates* was one of the books in our classroom library. Skating sounded like ever so much fun, gliding over the ice without hardly working at it. I had also watched kids skating on the little pond in town and it looked easy, too—just put the skates on and away you go.

"Ice skates?" Mom said. "Why do you want ice skates. We don't even have a pond."

"Yes we do," Dad answered. "Not a pond, I suppose, but what about the lake when we go ice fishing?"

Whenever I thought about skating and wondered where I would be able to go, I had always figured that somehow, I would have to convince Mom to let me flood part of the lawn to make a skating rink. One boy at school had done that. He said he had turned on the hose and let it run on the lawn, and then when the water froze, he had a place to go skating.

I had never once thought about the lake. Of *course* I could go skating on the lake when Dad and I went ice fishing. Later on in December—depending upon how cold the weather had been—and then in January and February, we would go ice fishing on Sunday afternoons, or sometimes on a Saturday. After Dad drilled the holes with a hand auger, there wasn't much to do unless the fish were biting. But, if I had ice skates with me, I could skate while we waited for the fish to bite.

"That's a good idea, Daddy," I said.

"Well," Mom said, "I don't know…"

"We'll just have to wait and see what Santa Claus finds," Loretta said.

A long time ago, I had figured out that Loretta was the one who bought gifts and wrapped them. Loretta knew that I knew, but she still insisted Santa Claus was the one who found the presents.

Since Mom and Loretta planned to go shopping on Saturday, we would have to do all of our house cleaning today. I would rather not dust and shake rugs and wash the steps a day early, but as Mom pointed out, if we finished our cleaning today, I could do whatever I wanted Saturday afternoon.

The next day after dinner, Mom and Loretta went shopping. They didn't ask me to go with them, but that was fine with me. I certainly did not want to stand around in a store while Loretta shopped, and it was either that, or sit in the car with Mom.

No, I would much rather be helping Dad, or playing with our dog, Needles, or riding my pony, Dusty.

Mom and Loretta came home later in the afternoon, and I tried to see if any of the packages looked like they might be ice skates, but none of the boxes seemed big enough. I wasn't worried, though. Christmas was still almost a month away.

Over the next several weeks, the pond in town called Mirror Lake froze enough so that when the buses left after school, I could see brightly dressed figures gliding around on the ice. The kids who lived in town could walk the couple of blocks to Mirror Lake, strap on their skates and start doing figure-eights in less time than it took to load the buses. While my bus stopped at the stop sign and waited for traffic on the highway, I often had a minute or two to watch the skaters.

Once I got my very own pair of skates, I knew I most likely would never go skating on Mirror Lake, but that didn't stop me from daydreaming about going skating when Dad and I went ice fishing. I could just picture it. There I'd be—sailing around in circles, skating far out across the lake and back again, skating so fast, the ends of my favorite bright blue scarf would fly out behind me. People who lived in the houses around the lake would watch from their windows and wonder about the identity of such an excellent and graceful skater.

A few days before Christmas, Dad and I cut the Christmas tree, and Loretta and I decorated it. I was so excited about my ice skates, I didn't even think about the possibility that I might not get skates for Christmas. And in fact, when we opened our gifts on Christmas Eve, one of the boxes with my name on it did, indeed, contain a pair of ice skates.

I pulled one of the skates out of the box. The white leather was just about the whitest thing I had ever seen. And the silver blades on the bottom were as bright and shiny as the stainless steel milker inflations after Dad or Ingman finished scrubbing them.

"What do you know about that? Ice skates!" my big brother said.

"Do you like them?" Loretta asked.

"Try them on, so we're sure they fit all right," Mom suggested.

I kicked off my slippers—great, big, pink, fuzzy ones that had been in another box with my name on it underneath the Christmas tree.

"I got them bigger than your regular shoe size so you can wear two or three pairs of socks in them," Loretta explained. "That way, I'm hoping you'll be able to use them for a couple of years instead of growing out of them right away."

I reached for the package of socks which had been one of my other presents. In my opinion, socks were the *worst* kind of Christmas present—although at least one package under the tree had contained socks every Christmas that I could remember. Mom said I wore socks out faster than anyone she ever knew. But then she would tell me that when she was a kid, she wore out socks fast, too. "My shoes would fit in the front, but they were loose in the back, and my stockings would wear out from sliding up and down against the shoes. You must have the same kind of foot," she'd say.

I put on two pairs of socks, a pink pair and a blue pair. The socks in the package were all different colors: red and pink and blue and yellow and light green. I slipped my foot into the skate.

"How does it feel?" Mom asked.

I wiggled my toes. "Too big," I said.

"Put on another pair of socks," Loretta said.

I pulled my foot out of the skate, slipped a yellow sock over my foot and put my foot back into the skate.

"Now how does it feel?" Loretta asked.

I wiggled my toes again. "Just right," I said.

"Good," Dad replied.

Up until now, my father hadn't said a word while I opened the skates and tried them on.

"When can we go ice fishing, Daddy?" I asked, as I started to put socks on my left foot so I could try on the other skate.

"I knew that question would be coming up pretty soon," he muttered.

"I'm on Christmas vacation, you know," I said. "We can go tomorrow!"

Dad shook his head. "No, we can't."

"Why not?"

I did not see any reason why we couldn't go ice fishing tomorrow. Since it was winter, Dad would not have any field work, not like in the summer when he was cultivating corn and soybeans or cutting and baling hay.

"It will be too cold outside tomorrow," Dad replied. "This morning the thermometer said fifteen below, and the weather forecast on the radio said it's supposed to be twenty below tomorrow morning."

Dad turned on the radio in the barn morning and evening because he said the cows liked music.

"So?" I said. "Won't it warm up in the afternoon?"

We always went ice fishing in the afternoon, anyway, after Dad had finished the chores.

"Not according to the radio," Dad said. "They say it will only warm up to zero and that there'll be a twenty-mile-an-hour north wind tomorrow. And if there's a twenty-mile-an-hour north wind, it will feel like it's twenty below in the afternoon yet. I don't know about you, but I'm not going to sit out on the ice when it's twenty below."

Now that he mentioned it, I could see his point. Just walking to barn was bad enough when it was twenty degrees below zero.

"You know how it goes in the winter. It will probably warm up soon," Loretta said, "and then you can try out your ice skates on the lake."

"In a few days, it might so warm that the snow is melting," Ingman said.

"Could be. You never know," Mom said.

Christmas Day the weather stayed cold. The day after Christmas, Loretta went back to work and would be staying at her apartment instead of coming home.

Those two days seemed more like a week, but finally on the third day, when I woke up in the morning, the thermometer said it was a whole two degrees *above* zero.

"Daddy! It's above zero this morning," I said when I got out to the barn. "Can we go ice fishing this afternoon?"

Dad shook his head. "The radio said it's going to start snowing this afternoon, and I'd rather not sit out in a snowstorm."

"Why not?"

"Because we'll get covered with snow, that's why. And there's no sense in being out in a snowstorm if we don't have to be."

One time during a snowstorm on a Saturday, the snow had started while Dad was hauling manure out to the field—heavy, wet flakes falling so thick and so fast, I could barely see the barn from the kitchen window. Dad said he had never seen it snow like that before, and by the time he came in the house, Mom said he looked like the abominable snowman.

The only abominable snowman I had ever seen was in *Rudolph the Red-nosed Reindeer* on television before Christmas. I didn't think Dad looked anything at all like the abominable snowman. Still, I could see that his coat and cap and the legs of his pants were dripping wet.

The snow started at mid-afternoon, and by the next morning, another eight inches covered the ground. The sun was shining, however, and the thermometer by the kitchen window said it was fifteen degrees.

When Dad came in for his morning coffee break, I decided I might as well ask.

"Daddy, can we go ice fishing this afternoon?"

My father shook his head. "No, we can't. I've got to get the tractor out and clear the snow from the driveway."

"Will that take all afternoon?" I asked.

"No, it won't. It will take the rest of the morning. I've got to move the snow first, then I'll have to clean the barn this afternoon."

Dad usually cleaned the barn in the morning. He would finish milking, eat breakfast, wash the milkers, wash the bulk tank, and then he would clean the barn.

The next day we couldn't go ice fishing, either, because we were almost out of cow feed. After Dad finished cleaning the barn, he was going to load the truck and take corn and oats to the feed mill to make more feed for the cows. If Ingman hadn't been working the day shift at the creamery, he could have taken the feed to town. But of course, he had been working the day shift all week.

By now, I had pretty much given up on going ice fishing so I could try out my skates before school started. My two weeks of Christmas vacation were almost over, and who wanted to try out some silly old skates, anyway? I should have asked for something else. Maybe a pair of skies. At least we had hills where I could use skies.

That evening, Loretta came home for the weekend, as she always did on Friday—unless there was a big snowstorm—and when we sat down at the supper table, I knew what I had to do.

"You can take my skates and get your money back," I said, as I looked down at my plate and turned my fork over and over.

"What?" Loretta said.

"What?" Mom asked.

"What?" Ingman wondered.

"Huh? What did you say?" Dad inquired.

I looked up and saw that all four of them were staring at me.

"I said, you can take my skates, Loretta, and get your money back."

"Why?" my sister said.

"Why?" Mom asked.

"Why?" Ingman wondered.

"Why do you want her to take your skates back?" Dad inquired.

"Because we don't have anywhere to skate right around here. It's dumb to have skates when there's no place to skate," I explained.

"I thought you were going to use your skates when you went ice fishing with Dad," Mom said.

"And why can't we go ice fishing tomorrow?" Loretta asked.

I stopped fidgeting with my fork and turned to look at my sister.

"'We'— what do you mean 'we.' You never go ice fishing," I said.

Once or twice in years past, Loretta had gone ice fishing with us. But she didn't fish. She would rather walk around and look at the scenery.

"Well, I'd like to go tomorrow," Loretta said. "I'm cooped up in an office all week, and it would be fun to get outside and do something."

I looked at Dad.

"Yes," he said, nodding slowly, "I suppose we could go tomorrow afternoon. After I'm done with all of the chores."

"Really?" I said.

"When I was feeding the cows before supper, the weather forecast said it's supposed to be in the twenties tomorrow, and sunny, so, yes, we can go ice fishing," Dad said.

All at once, my appetite came back. "We're going ice fishing!" I said, as I reached for the bowl of mashed potatoes.

The next day, when we had finished cleaning the house and Dad had finished all of the chores and we had eaten dinner, my father started gathering what we would need to go ice fishing.

"Why are we taking a snow shovel, Daddy?" I asked.

He lifted the snow shovel and pointed to the lawn. "See all of the snow there in the yard?"

This week we had gotten eight inches, and that was on top of the twelve inches which had fallen the week before.

"There will be that much snow on top of the ice too. We'll have to shovel a spot if we want to fish," Dad explained.

An hour later, after I had put on a pair of leotards under my corduroy pants and had wrapped my favorite bright blue scarf around my neck, and Loretta had found an extra sweater to wear under her coat, and Dad had looked in the closet until he located his wool felt ice fishing cap complete with ear flaps, we arrived at the place called Northwest Landing.

"Boy," Dad said as he turned to drive down the hill toward the lake, "am I ever glad to see they've put sand on the road. Otherwise we might not get back up again."

Sometimes my sister and I went swimming at Northwest Landing in the summer, but the lake looked very different now, white and sparkling in the sunshine, with a road plowed across it.

Dad drove to the boat landing and maneuvered the car onto the ice.

"Is it safe to drive on?" Loretta asked.

"With all the cold weather we've had, there's probably two feet of ice," Dad said.

My father soon stopped the car and turned off the ignition. "It's deep here, so we don't have to go too far out," he said.

Before we left home, I had asked why we weren't taking the pickup truck. Dad said without a load in the back, the truck wouldn't have enough traction to get up the hill from the lake. I knew what he meant. Sometimes the pickup tires would spin when we were trying to get up our driveway at home, too.

"Oh," Loretta said, turning in a circle, "it's so pretty with the sunshine and the snow."

The lake spread out around us like a giant piece of the white cottony material speckled with silver glitter that the Ladies Aid had put beneath our Christmas tree at church to keep the spruce needles off the floor.

"Yeah, snow's pretty all right," Dad said as he took the shovel out of the trunk. "Too bad there's so much of it."

My father went to work shoveling out a small area so he could drill a hole in the ice. Then he handed the shovel to me.

"Here you go, kiddo," he said. "You'll have to clear a spot so you can skate."

I looked at the shovel and then at Dad.

"Why can't I skate on the road?"

"The road's got a couple inches of packed snow. You've got to have clear ice to skate on," he said.

"Oh," I said.

I stuck the blade into the snow and lifted the shovel. I heaved five shovels of snow to one side. And then I stopped to rest. The snow was much heavier than it looked.

"Here," Loretta said, "give me the shovel. I'll help. We can take turns."

The snow piled higher and higher around us as we worked to clear a skating rink. Finally, after trading the shovel back and forth between us for a half an hour, and after taking several rest stops, a small, square area had been carved out in the snow.

"You've got about ten feet in both directions," Dad observed. "I think you'll have to learn how turn corners right away, or you won't get much skating done."

Seeing as my skating rink was ready, I could put on my skates.

"Sit *in* the car to do that. Don't just open the door and sit sideways," Dad said. "That way, you won't have even a chance to get your socks wet in the snow."

Minutes later, my skates were on and laced and tied. I opened the car door and stood up. Standing on skates was weird. For one thing, I was taller. And for another thing, I only had a narrow strip of steel on which to balance. I took a careful step. And then another one.

Walking with skates on, I decided, was easy, and a few steps later, I reached my skating rink.

I took another step forward onto the area we had cleared of snow.

One second, I was upright.

The next second, my legs were stretched out in front of me, and I was sitting on the freezing cold ice.

"Are you all right?" Loretta said, hurrying toward me. She was wearing a pair of light blue pants—the color made me think of blue jay feathers—with straps that went under her feet so the pants stayed inside her short brown leather boots.

"I think so," I said, trying to determine what I should do with my legs and feet so I could stand up.

"Here," Loretta said, holding out one hand covered with a brown leather glove.

I took hold of my sister's hand, but when I was halfway up, both feet shot out from under me.

It took a while, but eventually, I was standing on my skates once more.

"Okay," Loretta said, "I think you should—"

Before she could finish her sentence, I was sitting on the ice again.

"Ouch!" I said. The first time, I hadn't come down this hard.

"I'm going to grab your hands and put my feet in front of yours. Maybe that will work better to help you stand up," my sister said.

Loretta's foot kept the skates from sliding forward, and in a few minutes, I was on my feet.

"I'm going to hold your hand to help you balance," Loretta said. "Try shuffling your feet to see if you can start moving—"

In spite of Loretta's grasp on my hand, I must have shuffled too much because this time, the skates shot out from beneath me *backwards*. I was so surprised that I let go of my sister's hand.

"Oof," I said, as I fell forward onto the ice.

Sometimes my mother said 'uff-da!,' which, as I understood it, was a Norwegian way of saying 'oh, my,' but I wasn't trying to say 'uff-da'—the 'oof' came as the breath was knocked out of my chest.

"Are you okay?" Loretta asked.

I nodded. "Wind…"

"What?"

"Wind…" I gasped.

"You've had the wind knocked out of you?" Dad asked.

I nodded again and looked up to see both Dad and Loretta staring down at me, an anxious expression on their faces.

I stayed there for a minute until I got my breath back, and then Dad and Loretta helped me stand up.

After I had landed on the ice for the sixth time, I stopped counting.

An hour later, Dad was ready to quit fishing because it was time to feed the cows and also because the fish weren't biting, and by then, I could skate the length of the rink—sort of—as long as Loretta kept a tight grip on my hand. At one point she let go, and—following a little bit of fancy footwork—down I went again.

Lucky for me we only lived a couple of miles from the lake because sitting in the car wasn't very comfortable.

Blue shadows had begun to creep across the snow as the sun moved lower on the horizon, and while we drove along, I kept shifting my position in the back seat to find a better way to sit. When we arrived at the farm, I slowly climbed out of the car, and with the box that held my skates tucked under my arm, I limped to the house. I set the box in the porch and opened the door into the kitchen.

"How was it?" Mom asked.

I took off my coat, hung it on the back of a kitchen chair, and pulled up the sleeve of my sweater. A lovely patch of purple had blossomed on my forearm.

"Ooooo...ouch. That looks painful," Mom said.

I pulled up my other sleeve, where another lilac-colored bruise was beginning to show. I was pretty sure my knees and shins had bruises, too.

"How many times did you fall down?" Mom asked.

I shook my head. "I don't know. I stopped counting after six."

"Six!" Mom exclaimed.

Loretta unzipped her coat and took off the fluffy blue stocking cap that matched her slacks. "I think it's like riding a bike. Once you get the hang of it, it suddenly becomes much easier," she said.

"I suppose it's like riding a horse, too," Mom said. "And you know what they say about riding a horse. When you fall off, you must get right back on. You will just have to keep trying with the skates."

I had taken several tumbles off Dusty, but never one right after another.

You know, all things considered, I can honestly say that ice skating was not *quite* as easy—or as much fun—as I had imagined it would be.

****

~ 13 ~
Happy New Year!

Today was the last day of the year. December 31. New Year's Eve. And as I sat by the kitchen table with a couple of Christmas cookies—cut-out sugar cookies with frosting because those were my favorite—I could hardly believe tonight was the big night.

Before this, I hadn't paid much attention to New Year's. To me, New Year's only meant Christmas vacation was almost over and that I would soon be going back to school. On New Year's Day, we ate a big dinner like the dinners we had for Thanksgiving or Christmas, and then in the afternoon, we took down the Christmas tree and put away the decorations.

And that was it for New Year's.

But this year, on one particularly cold afternoon during Christmas vacation when it was too cold to go sledding and definitely too cold to ride my pony, Dusty, I had started looking through Loretta's magazines for something to do. The January issues of the women's magazines to which my sister subscribed had showed up in the mail a week or two before Christmas, and as I paged through them, I discovered they contained articles about New Year's.

Some of the articles talked about a big New Year's Eve celebration in Times Square in New York City and that people from all over the world would come to New York to watch the ball drop at midnight.

I had no idea what that meant—to watch the ball drop in Times Square. Mom said it meant what it sounded like. A big ball would be suspended high above the street in New York City. A square, Mom said, was an open space in the middle of town, and the one in New York City was called Times Square. As midnight approached, people would start counting, and the ball would begin its journey to the ground. It would reach the bottom precisely at the stroke of midnight, she said.

The articles also mentioned that people threw confetti.

I had never heard of confetti, so I looked it up in the dictionary and found out confetti was bits of paper or ribbon people threw around to celebrate an event.

The articles said, too, that people blew horns, sang songs and laughed and danced because they were so happy about New Year's Eve.

Another strange thing I found out was that some people waited in Times Square *all day*.

If people waited *all day*, New Year's Eve must be something really special. I couldn't imagine what it would be like to wait outside in any kind of weather *all day* for one single event. Even the ten or fifteen minutes I waited for a sheet of cookies to come out of the oven when Loretta was baking cookies seemed like an eternity to me.

The more I found out about New Year's Eve in Time's Square, the more interesting it sounded.

I knew I would never have a chance to see the ball drop on New Year's Eve in Time's Square, though. We lived in Wisconsin, and according to the map in the *World Book Encyclopedia*, New York City was a long, long, *long* ways away.

But then I came across a bit of information about New Year's Eve that made me sit up and take notice.

The New Year's Eve celebration in Time's Square, the article said, would be broadcast on television.

At midnight.

I had never in my entire life stayed up until midnight.

"Mom!" I said.

"What?" my mother asked. She was sitting by the desk in the living room, black rimmed reading glasses on, going through receipts and records to get ready for filing Income Taxes. When Mom talked about Income Taxes, the words sounded like they were in capital letters.

"It says that the ball dropping in Times Square will be on television," I said.

"Yes," Mom said, as she pulled another receipt out of an envelope, "I knew that."

"You *knew*?"

My mother nodded as she put the receipt on one of the piles in front of her.

I drew a couple of deep breaths. "Would it—I mean—could I—I mean, can I...errr...*may* I stay up and watch it?"

Mom peered at me through her glasses. "Well...that's awfully late."

"Please, Mom? Pretty please? With sugar on top?"

She took off her glasses and laid them on the desk. "I suppose staying up late for once wouldn't hurt you."

She held up one finger.

"But—only if you turn the volume down. And only if you shut off all the lights in the house. You can plug that little night light in out in the kitchen. The one we got when you had your Halloween party. The rest of us have to get some sleep, you know."

Mom and Dad went to bed on New Year's Eve the same time they did any other night. They never stayed up late to see New Year's. Dad woke up at 5:30 every morning so he could get out to the barn to start the chores. He said he didn't mind that the new year arrived when he was sleeping because he would see it soon enough, anyway.

"Thanks, Mom!" I said.

My mother picked up her glasses. "Just remember what I told you about the lights and the volume on the television."

Even though I was happy about getting permission to watch the ball drop in Time's Square, I did not want the rest of Christmas vacation to go by *too* quickly. So, over the next several days, I tried not to think about New Year's Eve.

But today, New Year's Eve had arrived. I finished eating my Christmas cookies, and although it was only mid-afternoon, I opened the catch-all drawer next to the stove to look for the night light. Mom said it sounded better to call it the 'catch-all drawer' rather than the 'junk drawer.' My sister had bought the night light before my Halloween party so that if my friends needed to use the bathroom in the middle of the night, they would be able to see their way across the kitchen. The clear bulb was shaped like a Christmas tree bulb and was screwed into a socket that plugged directly into the outlet.

The only time we had used the night light was during my Halloween party, and when I found it in the drawer, I set it on the counter between the kitchen sink and the wall where the old butter-yellow Time-A-Trol clock kept track of the hours.

My next step in preparing for New Year's Eve was to go upstairs and find an extra blanket. We kept a blanket folded up on the couch for those times when the living room felt chilly. I would need an extra blanket because the woodstove would be down to coals when midnight approached, and I didn't want to be shivering while I was watching New Year's Eve on television.

I pulled another blanket out of the trunk upstairs, took it to the living room and set it on top of the blanket folded up on the davenport. *Now* I was ready for New Year's Eve.

Later in the evening, after we had finished the milking, and Dad and I had returned to the house, and we had washed our hands and faces, Mom, Dad, Loretta and I sat by the table to eat a bowl of strawberry swirl ice cream. Strawberry swirl was Mom's favorite.

"Look what I found at the store!" Loretta said, reaching into the back of the refrigerator. She turned around and held out a glass jar.

'Fudge Marshmallow Ice Cream Topping' the label said.

"We hardly ever have ice cream topping!" I exclaimed.

My sister set the jar on the counter and opened the drawer to find a spoon. "I thought it might be nice to have a special treat on New Year's Eve," she said.

Dad dished up the ice cream, and Loretta put spoonfuls of Fudge Marshmallow Ice Cream Topping on the scoops of strawberry swirl in each bowl.

"Oh, yum, that looks good," Mom said when Loretta set a bowl down in front of her.

I had finished my third spoonful of strawberry swirl with Fudge Marshmallow Ice Cream Topping when the yawn snuck up on me. I quickly put my hand over my mouth. Mom said it was impolite to yawn without covering your mouth.

"You're not tired already, are you?" Mom asked.

Loretta turned her head to look at the kitchen clock. "It's more than two hours until midnight," she said.

"No," I said, "I'm not sleepy."

And, in fact, I did not feel sleepy. I had no idea where the yawn came from.

"Course she's not tired," Dad said as he lifted another spoonful of ice cream out of the bowl, "she's staying up until midnight to see New Year's come in."

I tried to take small spoonfuls, but eating a bowl of ice cream never lasted long enough, and when I had scraped up the last of the Strawberry Swirl and the Fudge Marshmallow Ice Cream Topping, I considered picking up the bowl and licking it out. Then I decided against it. I knew what Mom would say. "You are not a dog. Young ladies do *not* lick out their bowls!"

We did have a dog, of course, but I could not let Needles lick out the bowl. Needles was not allowed to stay in the house. During the day, he came in and went out with Dad, but at night, he stayed outside. Dad wanted him to sleep in the barn, where it was warmer, but Needles did not want to be locked in the barn. If Dad tried shutting the dog in the barn after the weather turned cold, Needles barked and yipped and howled until Dad let him out. My father made a bed of old burlap feed sacks in the granary for Needles and then left the door open a little bit so the dog could go in and out as he pleased. The arrangement seemed to suit Needles, but I worried about him when the weather stayed below zero for days at a time.

I set my bowl in the sink and turned on the tap to rinse it out. Mom said ice cream bowls were hard to wash when they were left to sit overnight without being rinsed. I looked at the kitchen clock and saw that it was almost time for the news. After Mom and Dad and Loretta watched the news and the weather, they would go to bed, and then my New Year's Eve would officially begin.

Before going into the living room, I went upstairs to get a book. I wasn't interested in listening to the news and the weather. I wanted to read more in my book while I waited for the news to finish. The book was about a girl named Katie John.

With my book tucked under my arm, I returned to the living room and saw that Dad had sat on the end of the davenport near the doorway to the kitchen, Loretta sat in the middle of the davenport and Mom was in her easy chair by the picture window.

The living room was already starting to feel chilly, so I wrapped a blanket around my shoulders and sat down on the far end of the davenport next to Loretta.

I had read ten pages when the weather report started. In a few minutes, as the weatherman finished the forecast, Mom reached for her crutches. "I'm going to bed," she said. "Remember what I told you about the volume and the lights?"

"Yes, Mom," I said. "I have to turn the television down low enough just so I can hear it. And I have to keep the lights off."

My mother stood up and made her way toward the kitchen. I put my bookmark in the book and threw back the blanket. I might as well go ahead and plug in the night light and turn it on.

In the middle of the sports report, Loretta went upstairs, and a few minutes later, Dad said goodnight and left the room, too. I had the

living room all to myself. I turned the volume knob down on the
television and went back to the davenport. Could I hear the television
well enough? I sat there for a minute and decided I could hear it well
enough. If it was too loud, I knew Mom would open the door that
connected their bedroom with the living room and would tell me to turn
it down more. I got up and switched off the lamp by Mom's chair, then
I went into the kitchen and turned off the light.

The house seemed so different with all of the lights off and only the
night light in the kitchen and the blue light of the television in the
living room.

I curled up on the davenport, reached for both blankets and then
paused as it dawned on me that a pillow might be a good idea. With a
heavy sigh, I flipped the blankets back, went into the kitchen and up the
stairs, grabbed a pillow off my bed and went back to the living room.

On television, a man was talking and telling jokes. I put the pillow
near the arm of the davenport and crawled under the blankets again.

Maybe, while I was waiting for New Year's Eve to start, I could
close my eyes for a few minutes. Midnight was more than an hour
away, so what difference would it make if I shut my eyes for a little
while...

I don't know how long I had been lying there with my eyes closed,
but all at once, it seemed like something was different in the room. My
eyelids snapped up, like window shades that had been let go too
quickly. But what was different?

The light. That's what was different. Instead of a man talking, many
people moved across the television screen, waving at each other and
blowing noisemakers that unrolled when they blew into them and rolled
up again when they stopped. I knew they were called noisemakers
because I had read about them in Loretta's magazines.

What time was it anyway?

I twisted around to look through the doorway into the kitchen. I
could barely see the clock and was about to get up when I remembered
Alice-in-Wonderland. I tipped my watch toward the light cast by the
television. It was 10:45.

And here I thought I had been asleep for hours. I must have only
dozed off for five minutes or so.

I settled down on the pillow again. People were still moving around
and waving and blowing their noisemakers, but the camera was focused

on a man with a microphone in his hand. I listened closely so I could catch what he was saying.

"As you can see folks, we have a fine crowd here in Times Square, waiting for midnight and the ball to drop. If you look over my shoulder..."

The camera turned toward the suspended ball. Mom was right. It really was a ball high above the street. A glittery, shiny ball.

"...you will see that the ball is ready to go when the countdown starts, although that won't be for a while yet," the man said.

I raised up on one elbow and reached behind me to fluff the pillow. It was a long time until midnight, and I might as well be comfortable while I waited.

I settled down once more and pulled the blankets up to my chin. The drone of the man's voice in the background made me think of bees buzzing on a warm summer day, and the people laughing and chattering and blowing noisemakers sounded a little like birds singing high in the trees. 'This is as nice as resting in the shade on a hot summer day,' I thought. 'It's a lot darker than a summer day, and colder, too, but..."

All at once, my eyes popped open.

"Four, three, two and HAPPY NEW YEAR!" shouted the announcer on television.

I rubbed my eyes and tried to focus on the television screen. The glittery ball was sitting on the ground, and an instrument, which I thought was probably a saxophone, began to play.

"Should old acquaintance be forgot and never brought to mind," sang the people on television.

'That must be the song they talked about in the article, *Auld Lang Syne*,' I thought while I struggled to sit up.

The camera swept back and forth over the crowd of people singing, laughing, dancing, throwing confetti and blowing noisemakers.

"As you can see," the announcer on television said, "the celebration continues. But that's all for our live coverage, folks. We'll see you next year. For those of you in Central Standard Time and on the west coast, here's wishing you a Happy New Year when it's midnight where you are."

When it's midnight where you are?

What did he mean by that?

I turned Alice-in-Wonderland toward the light from the television. It was 11:05.

Wait a minute.

If the ball was sitting on the ground, that meant they had already dropped the ball in Times Square, so that must mean I had missed New Year's. Except—how could they drop the ball in Times Square when it wasn't even midnight?

I thought about it for a minute or two.

Then I figured it out.

Although it was midnight in New York when they dropped the ball in Times Square—it was an hour earlier in Wisconsin because of the time zone difference. Midnight in New York was only 11 o'clock in Wisconsin.

I was thinking about how I had missed New Year's but yet at the same time had not missed New Year's, when I realized I was almost falling asleep sitting up. I tossed the blankets back, turned off the television and headed into the kitchen.

On my way through the kitchen, I glanced at the old Time-A-Trol clock hanging on the wall. And then I thought of something else.

Not only had I missed the ball dropping in Times Square, but I also would not be staying up until midnight. I was much too tired for that.

And as I climbed the steps toward my room—somehow—I still couldn't see what was so special about New Year's Eve.

****

Off Like a Shot...

The sun was so bright that sparkles shimmered on the snow as I stood at the top of the pasture hill, holding the tow rope for the toboggan made of red painted strips and varnished wood. The toboggan, which reminded me of a candy cane, was a smaller version of the long toboggans with curled over fronts. I had gotten the toboggan for Christmas last year, and the very first time I had tried it, I realized that sliding in the pasture was fun.

Before I got the toboggan, I had gone sledding on our driveway, and when the snow was packed from the weight of the car and the pickup truck and the milk truck traveling up and down the hill, my sled would go all the way to the bottom of the driveway and across the road.

That is, I had used the sled on the driveway until Mom insisted I slide in the pasture next to the driveway.

One car a week might go past our driveway during the winter. Sometimes the road beyond our place was plowed and sometimes it was not. No one lived up the road from us, and our farm and the next-door neighbor's place were the only two farms along our road. But even though few cars traveled the mile-long stretch of country road, my mother still worried about cars when I slid down the driveway.

As I soon discovered, my sled did not work very well in the deep snow covering the pasture. And if I went over a tuft of dry, brown pasture grass or a frozen pocket gopher mound, sometimes the runners would stick, and on more than one occasion when my sled stopped abruptly, I had landed face down in the snow.

After I got the toboggan last year, I found out I couldn't even tell when I went over tufts of grass and gopher mounds. Sliding on the fluffy snow was as much fun as riding on a magic carpet. I had never actually ridden on a magic carpet, of course, but the toboggan was as much as I imagined a magic carpet would be. Sledding down the driveway, after I thought about it, was a hard and bumpy experience, especially when my sled veered off to one side, hit the snowbank, and I tumbled onto the ground.

But—that was last year—and this was this year—and over the past few weeks, it came to my attention that sliding with my toboggan was not as much fun as it used to be.

With the toe of my boot, I nudged the toboggan until it was poised on the brink of the hill. I tossed the tow rope onto the front, sat down, rocked back and forth and pushed on the ground with my mittened hands.

Nothing happened.

I rocked back and forth some more and kept pushing.

Still nothing happened.

On the third try, the toboggan inched forward, and I began another trip down the hill.

In the time that it took to slide to the bottom, I could have hopped off at the top, ran down the hill and waited for my toboggan to arrive.

The toboggan finally reached the bottom of the hill and came to a slow and gentle halt.

Last year, and earlier this year, too, the toboggan had often traveled down the hill so fast that instead of stopping at the bottom, it went part of the way up the other hill toward the driveway.

But not anymore.

I put my feet down, one on each side of the toboggan, and stood up. Instead of turning around and climbing to the top the hill behind me so I could make another trip down, I climbed the hill in front of me, crawled through fence and pulled my toboggan out onto the driveway.

I stood on the driveway and was tempted slide down the hill to see if my toboggan was any faster here than in the pasture, but then I thought maybe I'd better not. I had promised Mom I wouldn't slide on the driveway anymore. And a promise, after all, *was* a promise. Mom said people who didn't keep their promises were people who could not be trusted. Dad said that people who were not as good as their promises were no good at all.

Besides, Mom was sitting in her chair by the picture window, and she would see me sliding down the driveway.

I wrapped the tow rope around my hand and headed up the hill toward the house. I rounded the curve at the top of the hill, and a clattering sound came from the machine shed followed by a series of tapping noises. The tapping stopped, and a loud crash made me wonder if someone had dropped all of the bolts stored under the workbench, although I thought it was more likely that Dad had hit something with his ball-peen hammer.

I trudged around the edge of the lawn and toward the machine shed, my toboggan bumping along behind me. When I reached the door, I dropped the tow rope and went inside. The difference between the bright sunshine sparkling on the snow and the dim interior of the machine shed made the shed seem as dark as it would be outside tonight when I went to the barn to feed the calves and carry milk.

My eyes started to adjust to the change in light after a few seconds, and I could see my father crouched beside the manure spreader, tools spread out around him on the concrete floor. Our dog, Needles, sat not far away, keeping a close eye on Dad. Needles glanced at me, and his white feathery tail slowly brushed back and forth across the floor behind him.

"Daddy?" I said.

Dad reached for a screwdriver without bothering to look up.

"What?" he said.

"My toboggan doesn't work."

My father turned the trouble light so he could see better.

"Daddy, didn't you hear me?"

"I don't know why this has to be so hard to do," Dad muttered. He slipped the end of the screwdriver into one of the links on the manure spreader chain, bent closer, set the screwdriver down and reached for another device that was flat on one end, like a screwdriver, but was larger than any of the screwdrivers nearby.

"Daddy?"

My father reached for the hammer. "If I tap it thus-and-so, that link ought to pop off there," he said.

'Thus-and-so' was one of Dad's favorite phrases. He used it when he was trying to accomplish a task but was not one hundred percent certain his idea would work.

Tap-tap-tap went the hammer.

"Almost," Dad muttered.

"Daddy, you're not listening to me."

"Why this doggone chain has to be about a half a link too long is beyond me," Dad said.

"But I suppose if I take a link out, then it will be too short," he added.

"Daddy!" I said.

"What?" My father paused and looked up.

"I said—my toboggan doesn't work."

Dad laid the hammer on the floor. "What do you mean, your toboggan doesn't work. Won't it go down the hill?"

"Well, yes, it goes down the hill—"

"I'm busy," Dad said abruptly. "Gotta get this manure spreader fixed so I can clean the barn. I'm behind as it is. I should've had the barn cleaned this morning, and now it's after dinner already."

Today was Sunday. Dad tried to arrange the cleaning schedule so he would not have to clean the barn on Sunday. If the weather was warm enough so the cows could go outside for the afternoon or even just for a few hours, then he would clean every other day, although when the cows stayed in most of the time, he cleaned the barn every day. Yesterday would have been his regular cleaning day, except that yesterday, the barn cleaner chain had broken, and he had to fix that first before he could clean the barn. Fixing the barn cleaner chain had taken most of the day. But this afternoon, the manure spreader wasn't working right, so he had to fix that, too, before he could clean the barn.

I turned to leave, head down, staring at the floor, scraping my boots against the concrete.

Behind me, I heard Dad sigh, and then I heard the clatter of the hammer as he dropped it on the floor.

"Oh, all right," he muttered. "I guess I can spare a few minutes. What's wrong with your toboggan?"

I whirled around and skipped back toward him. "My toboggan won't go fast, Daddy!"

Dad rubbed his hand against the whiskers on his jaw. He shaved every day, unless he had so much work to do that he elected to skip shaving so he could save a few minutes and get back to work that much sooner.

"Won't go fast, huh? It works all right but it's slow?" he asked.

I nodded.

"Hmmmmmm," he said.

When he stood up, Needles stood up, too, and when Dad went outside, Needles followed.

I hurried out the door and was just in time to see Dad pick up the tow rope and start for the house, pulling my toboggan behind him.

"Where are you going?" I asked as I trotted to catch up.

"Can't fix it out here. It's too cold," he said.

We arrived at the steps, and Dad stood my toboggan on end and brushed the snow off the bottom. He carried the toboggan up the steps, through the porch and into the kitchen, where he set it against the table.

My father took off his chore cap, hung it on the newel post and unzipped his coat. As he hung his coat in the porch, my mother made her way into the kitchen from the living room.

"Why on earth are you bringing that in here?" Mom asked, looking at the toboggan propped against the kitchen table.

"Gotta fix it," Dad explained. He laid the toboggan upside-down on the rug in front of the kitchen sink.

"Fix it?" my mother said. "Is it broken?'

Dad opened the cabinet under the kitchen sink and began pushing aside bottles and scrub pails and piles of cleaning rags.

"What *are* you looking for?" Mom inquired.

Dad shut the cupboard door and held up a green bottle.

"T-u-r-t-l-e-W-a-x" was printed on the label.

It was the same bottle of Turtle Wax that Dad used in the spring to wax the 460 Farmall.

I knew why Dad waxed the tractor. He said waxing the tractor would help protect the paint from the hot sun while he was doing the field work.

What I couldn't figure out was why he would need wax for my toboggan.

"What's that for?" I asked.

"The bottom of your toboggan," he replied.

"Look here," Dad said. He turned the toboggan over. "See how the varnish is nice and bright on the top side?"

I knelt down on the floor beside him. The top of my toboggan was bright and shiny with varnish, like the windowsills in the living room were bright and shiny with varnish.

"But look at the other side," he said, turning the toboggan over.

The bottom of the toboggan was not nearly as bright and shiny as the top side.

I turned to face Dad.

"How is wax going to help my toboggan?" I asked.

Wax, I knew, felt sticky when it was wet. After it dried, it felt like the chalk dust on the erasers at school, except that it was still a bit sticky. Once the wax was wiped off, however, you couldn't tell it had been there.

"How will it help your toboggan?" Dad said. "Wait and see."

I watched as Dad poured wax on the bottom of the toboggan and spread it around with his fingers. The smell of the wax made me think of the almond extract my sister used for baking cookies. He finished smearing on the wax, and the bottom of the toboggan was covered with a thick layer of pasty-looking white.

Dad stood up, rinsed his hands and dried them on the hand towel Mom kept on the towel bar by the kitchen sink next to the dish towels.

Dish towels, my mother said, were meant for drying dishes, and hand towels were meant for drying hands. I had been in trouble a couple of times for wiping my hands on the dish towel, and I wondered if Dad had gotten into trouble over the same thing, because I noticed that if he washed his hands at the sink, he was careful to dry his hands on the hand towel.

Dad dried his hands, picked up the toboggan and set it against the wall behind furnace grate in the floor that took up one corner of the kitchen. The furnace was directly below the floor, and when the pilot light ignited and all the burners were going, the heat came directly up into the kitchen.

Sometimes, if the temperature was below zero outside and my coat and boots were frosty from sitting in the porch, I would set them on the furnace grate to take the chill off before I put them on. Mom said we had that kind of furnace because the house was so old it didn't pay to put in duct work.

When I asked what duct work was, Dad had explained that ducts looked like big tubes installed under the floor to carry heat to different rooms in the house. Our furnace, he said, worked by radiant heat. I asked what radiant meant, and Mom said it was like the woodstove in the living room—the heat simply moved out into the room the way sunshine radiated down from the sky and warmed the earth. The furnace worked well enough to keep the kitchen, bathroom and Mom and Dad's bedroom warm. Less of the heat made it upstairs. But hardly any of the heat carried into the living room, which is why we had a woodstove in the living room.

While we waited for the toboggan to dry, Dad and I sat down at the table and ate some of the cookies Loretta had baked yesterday. My sister said they were called Snickerdoodles. I giggled when she told me what they were called. Snickerdoodles was a funny name for cookies, in my opinion, although there was nothing funny about the way they tasted. Snickerdoodles, I discovered when I ate my first one, were a kind of sugar cookie dipped in sugar and cinnamon.

By the time we finished our cookies and Dad had finished his cup of coffee, the wax was dry. Dad used one of Mom's cleaning rags to wipe the dry wax off the bottom of my toboggan.

"Come on, kiddo," he said, zipping up his coat.

My father waited while I put on my coat, boots, hat and mittens. He carried my toboggan outside and set it on the ground. I hurried to catch up with him, and a few minutes later, Dad crawled through the fence next to driveway and positioned my toboggan at the top of the slope. I rarely slid in this direction because the hill was higher on the other side of the pasture, but I supposed that for once, to see how my toboggan worked, I could slide down the shorter slope.

"Hop on," Dad instructed as he stood next to the toboggan, holding the tow rope. Needles had followed us out to the pasture. He never ventured into deep snow by himself because his legs were so short. But, since Dad had crawled through the fence, Needles crawled through the fence, too.

I sat down on the toboggan, and Dad gave me the tow rope.

I leaned forward to put my hands on the ground so I could push to get myself started—and the toboggan shot off down the hill.

Needles, who had come around to the front of the toboggan, leaped out of the way with a startled 'woof!"

I reached the bottom of the short hill, got off my toboggan and pulled it back to where Dad was standing.

"Is that better?" he asked.

"Oh, yes, Daddy! Much better!"

"Good," Dad said, "because I have *got* to get that manure spreader fixed so I can clean the barn. It will be time to feed the cows in not too long."

Dad headed toward the machine shed, and I climbed the opposite hill to try out my toboggan from that part of the pasture. At the top of the slope, I sat down, leaned forward—and held onto the tow rope for dear life, my cheeks tingling with the cold, as the toboggan raced to the bottom of the hill and part way up the next slope toward the fence.

Again and again, I pulled my toboggan to the top of the hill so I could slide down, and after a while, on one trip to the top, I saw Dad drive the tractor and manure spreader to the back of the barn so he could start cleaning. I was glad my father had fixed the manure spreader, but I didn't have much time to think about it as my toboggan flew down the hill once more.

For a long time, I had known wax was good for cars and trucks and tractors, but I never dreamed that it could be good for toboggans, too.

No wonder I was convinced that Dad could fix anything.

****

~ 15 ~
The Skating Party

When the Girl Scout leaders announced one winter day that our next meeting would be a skating party at the pond in town, I made up my mind I was going to skip the next Girl Scout meeting. Or at least, I thought I was going to skip Girl Scouts—until Mom found out about the party. I might have known the Girl Scout leaders would not stop with merely telling us about the skating party. No. They also sent out a letter through the mail.

"Well," Mom said as I took off my coat and hung it up in the closet. "I see that you're having a skating party for Girl Scouts!"

I had learned of the skating party two days ago. But as I walked up the hill after getting off the school bus just now, I was not thinking about skating. I tried very hard not to think about skating. Putting on skates was a disaster I did not care to repeat. Not after the first time I had used the new skates I got for Christmas and discovered I couldn't even stand up, much less skate.

"How do you know we're having a skating party?" I asked, pulling out a chair by the kitchen table to sit down.

"It says so right here," Mom said. She held up the letter. "The Girl Scout leaders wrote a letter to each of the mothers so we would know the date, the time, the place and what you're supposed to bring for the party."

Only a dozen girls belonged to the group, but we had two Girl Scout leaders: one with sandy-reddish hair and one with dark hair. Both of them went out of their way to make sure we always had fun during our Girl Scout meetings. Up to now, that is.

My mother laid the letter on the table, looked at me and frowned.

"Why didn't you say anything about the skating party?" she asked.

I swallowed hard and tried to think of a good answer.

"Because I forgot?" I said.

"You forgot? How could you forget a thing like that? It's a party!"

"I don't know. I forgot."

"Young lady, I don't think you forgot. What I'm thinking is that you don't want to go."

I wasn't aware that I had been holding my breath until a faint sigh escaped through my lips. Maybe this wasn't going to be so hard after all. Maybe she really did understand.

My sense of relief evaporated in an instant, however, when my mother tapped the letter with one finger.

"You signed up for Scouts, and you are going to that party," she said.

"But Mom," I protested, "it's a *skating* party, and I'm still black and blue from the last time." Which was true. Bruises on my knee and on my elbow hadn't quite faded away from my first experience with skating almost two weeks ago. The other bruises had already healed.

"You are a member of Girl Scouts, and that means you have an obligation to participate in the activities," my mother said. "What good is it to join if you're not going to take advantage of it?"

I opened my mouth to respond, although I had no idea what I intended to say.

"And that's another thing," she continued. "You wanted those skates, but now you don't want to learn how to use them?"

"Well, no…it's not that I don't want to learn. It's that I keep falling down."

"You know what they say—'practice makes perfect,'" my mother said. "How are you going to learn to use your skates if you don't actually put the skates on and try?"

"I *did* try!" I said.

"Once," Mom replied. "Going out and using your skates *once* when you went ice fishing with Dad does not give you much practice. There will be other girls at the party, too, who won't know how to skate very well."

"They all know how to skate," I said.

"How do you know?"

"Because they've been talking about the party, and they all say they know how to skate."

"Be that as it may, you are going to the skating party, and that's that," Mom said.

I knew from the tone of my mother's voice—like it or not—I was going to the skating party.

I also knew it was going to be the worst day of my life.

On the morning of the next Girl Scout meeting, I found myself lugging my ice skates to school, along with two dozen cookies that would be part of our snack afterward. The letter from the Girl Scout leaders said they would provide hot chocolate and that each of the girls should bring something to share with other Scouts. Loretta had baked her special chocolate chip cookies last weekend. They were made with a whole cup of butter and two packages of milk chocolate chips. I liked milk chocolate better than semi-sweet because the semi-sweet tasted bitter, I thought.

"Have fun at your skating party," Mom said as I headed out the door to catch the bus.

"And remember, 'practice makes perfect,'" she added.

I was riding the bus to school, but I would not be coming home on the bus. Dad would drive into town to bring me home later this afternoon.

On any other school day, the hours seemed to drag by. I would sit and look out the window at the sunshine and think about how much fun I could be having with my toboggan if I was at home, and then I would look at the clock and see that even though it seemed like an hour must have gone by, it was only a couple of minutes.

But today, every time I looked at the clock, an hour had gone by, even though it seemed like only a few minutes, and the final bell rang long before I wanted it to.

I slowly put on my coat and boots and hat and mittens. My arms and legs felt as if they each weighed as much as the pails of milk I carried to the milkhouse while Dad and I were doing the chores, and as I fumbled with the zipper on my coat, the other girls were already dressed and were waiting for me.

"Come on!" one girl said impatiently. "What's taking you so long?"

"Nothing," I said. "I have to get my skates. And the cookies."

I reached up into the coat closet to retrieve the box that held my skates. I set the skates on a nearby desk and turned around to get the small paper bag three-quarters full of chocolate chip cookies. I tucked the skates under one arm and carried the cookies with my other hand.

"Good! Now we can go," said the Girl Scout who had asked me what was taking so long.

On Girl Scout meeting days, we usually wore our green Girl Scout uniforms to school, but seeing as we were going skating, we all were wearing regular winter clothes. Our boots scuffed against the polished tiles under our feet as we walked along the hall. At the end of the hall, the girl first in line pushed open the door, and we all followed her out onto the sidewalk.

Instead of bright and sunny, as it had been this morning, the afternoon sky was cloudy. The sidewalk next to the school soon turned into the sidewalk along the street. A raw wind swirled around us, and the other Girl Scouts chattered among themselves about the fun we would have at our skating party, although not *all* of them were talking about how much fun we would have. After a while, as I shifted the box with my skates from one arm to the other and transferred the cookies to the opposite hand, I noticed a couple of girls were not carrying skates.

Eventually another Girl Scout saw, too, that several members of the group were not carrying boxes or paper bags or did not have skates dangling over their shoulders.

"How come you guys don't have skates?" she asked.

One of the girls without skates shook her head. "I've never skated before. I don't have any," she said.

"Then how are you going to skate?" asked another girl.

"The leaders said we could use their daughters' old skates," she explained.

Less than a minute later, we stopped at the curb, looked both ways, crossed the street, and then—up ahead—I could see the pond.

A steep bank took us from the street to the edge of the frozen water. Dozens of skaters wearing bright blue or red or pink or purple or white winter coats skated in circles or up and down the length of the pond. So many feet had traveled from the street to the ice and back again that not one inch of snow was without footprints. We stood on the bank, looking at the skaters, and I wondered how we were ever going to find our Girl Scout leaders in the crowd of people.

I set my box of skates on the ground, turned toward the pond again and there, skating gracefully toward us, was the leader with dark hair. She was dressed in a beige jacket and black pants. From a distance, you couldn't tell her apart from the high school kids who were out skating.

"Oh, good," she said. "You're here. The skates for you girls are over there. Put your skates on and let's get started."

A short distance away stood a brown paper grocery bag with handles.

"But I don't know how to skate," said one of the girls who hadn't brought skates.

The leader smiled. "That's okay," she said. "I will teach you. I've taught lots of girls how to skate."

"Can you teach me, too?" asked another girl. "I just got my skates for Christmas."

"And me, too?"

"And me?"

I turned to look at them. Underneath the red-yellow-blue-and-white-striped stocking cap pulled low on my forehead, my eyebrows drew together in a frown. From the way they had talked about the party to begin with, I thought they *all* knew how to skate.

The Girl Scout leader laughed and adjusted the white knitted scarf looped around her neck. "Of course, I can teach you how. Listen carefully to my instructions, and I will do what I can to help you."

"Yipeeee!" said one girl. "I'm going to learn how to skate!"

"Me, too!" said another.

A glimmer of hope flickered in the back of my mind. If a couple of the other girls had never tried skating before, maybe I would not be the only one who couldn't stand up on skates.

I sat down on the snow, took off my boots, put on my skates and stood up. The packed snow provided enough traction so I could easily walk to the edge of the pond.

"Hey," said one of the other girls who had not brought skates, "this is easy. A lot easier than I thought!"

I was about to tell her that, sure, walking on the packed snow was easy—when she stepped off the low bank and onto the icy surface of the pond. She only took one step forward before her right foot went in one direction and her left went in the other. And then she was sitting on the ice, a surprised expression on her face.

"Ha-ha-ha!" said one of the girls who had also gotten skates for Christmas. "You can't even stand—"

Before the word 'up' was out of her mouth, her feet flew out from beneath her, and then she, too, was sitting on the ice.

One of the other Girl Scouts, who had been skating figure-eights, headed in our direction. "Are you all right?" she asked as she came to a halt by the two girls sitting on the ice.

"Yeah, I'm fine," said one.

"Me, too," said the other.

"Here, let me help you up," said the girl who was so good at skating figure-eights.

She pulled first one girl to her feet, then the other.

"Maybe if you hang onto each other, it will be easier to stand up," she said.

The girls stood face to face and held hands.

"Don't move," said one.

"I won't," promised the other.

I drew a deep breath and carefully stepped off the bank, putting first my right foot down on the ice and then the left.

I wasn't sure what happened next, though, because all of a sudden, I, too, was sitting on the ice.

"If you can get up and make it over here, then we can all three hold hands," said one of the girls.

I looked at the girls, and then I began to crawl toward them on my hands and knees. They were only a short distance away.

"Here," said one girl, holding out her hand.

Somehow, I got on my feet, and when I was standing, I took hold of the other girl's hand.

"Oh, this is much better when we're holding hands," said one of them.

The other girls who borrowed skates from the Scout Leader saw that we were staying on our feet by holding hands, so they held hands, too.

All around us, the remaining Girl Scouts were gliding back and forth, skating in circles and making figure-eights. The leader with sandy-reddish hair was skating with them.

"The first thing you need to do," said the Scout leader with dark hair as she skated toward us, "is to forget that you're wearing skates. Pretend you're wearing boots, instead."

"Boots?" one girl said doubtfully.

"If you think about the skates, you'll tense your muscles," the Scout leader said. "Pretend you're sliding your feet forward with boots on. And don't hold hands. If one falls down, you'll all fall down."

Reluctantly, we each went our separate ways.

I tried sliding my feet forward, the way I did when I was sliding with my boots on—which Mom said I should not do because I would wear my boots out before winter was over—and much to my surprise, I moved forward a little bit.

Without falling down.

Half an hour later, we were ready to eat our cookies and bars and to drink hot chocolate out of the thermos bottles the Scout leaders had brought, and I had managed to skate slowly halfway across the pond and back.

I had also managed to acquire a bunch of new bruises, although I wasn't alone. The other girls who had gotten skates for Christmas or who had borrowed skates from the Girl Scout leader also had gotten some new bruises.

We finished the hot chocolate and all of the cookies and bars, too, and then it was time to go home. My father arrived and parked the car by the curb above the pond. I picked up my box of skates, climbed the hill and opened the car door.

"Are ya cold, kiddo?" Dad asked as I pulled the door closed and settled back against the seat.

"I didn't feel cold while I was skating—"

And in the space of a breath, I realized what I had said.

"Dad! I was skating!"

He turned to look at me, and his right eye closed in a quick wink. "You were skating!"

"Actually, I didn't skate very far. And not very fast. And I still fell down. But maybe not as much as I did the first time."

"It's a start," Dad said as he pulled away from the curb and we headed for home.

"Did you have fun at your skating party?" Mom asked when I walked into the house fifteen minutes later.

I stopped to consider the question. I had been so busy trying to stand up on my skates, I hadn't thought about whether I was having fun.

"It was *sort* of fun, I guess. I skated a little bit. Not very far. And not very fast."

"See?" Mom said. "What did I tell you?"

I pushed up my sleeve to reveal a new bruise on my forearm. "But I thought you said practice makes perfect," I replied. "I still fell down—a lot."

"Practice *does* make perfect. You just have to keep working at it," she said.

"Are you sure?"

"I'm sure," Mom said. "I am one-hundred percent positive."

I looked at my mother without saying anything.

"Of course there's only one way to find out if I *am* right about practicing," Mom added.

"What's that?"

"To keep practicing," she replied.

Throughout the rest of the winter, we had two more Girl Scout skating parties, and I also brought my skates along when Dad and I went ice fishing. But in spite of hours and hours of trying, I never did learn to skate very well.

Wouldn't you just know it.

Mom *would* have to be wrong about skating.

Because as I found out the hard way—practice does not always make perfect.

****

Pete and Ole

Dad finished pouring a cup of coffee and gathered a handful of oatmeal cookies from the rows spread out on the cutting board to cool. After Mom baked bread or cake, or when Loretta baked cookies or pies or bars, they pulled the cutting board out from its slot beneath the kitchen counter and used it as a place to set the pans they had taken out of the oven. And then the cutting board stayed pulled out until the baking had cooled. My mother also used the cutting board to slice bread, of course, which anybody could see by the dozens of thin lines scored into its surface from the sharp knife edges.

I helped myself to two cookies and sat by the table next to Dad.

"It's no wonder I have to bake cookies every time I turn around," Loretta grumbled. She frowned and tried to look fierce and grumpy, but it didn't work. It never did. With her dark curly hair and smiling blue eyes, she was too pretty to look fierce and grumpy.

Dad shrugged and picked up another cookie. "Can't help myself. These cookies are awwww-ful good."

Loretta often baked cookies on Sunday afternoons, and she was in the middle of making a triple batch of oatmeal. She would take some of the cookies with her when she left for her apartment later today.

"What's that book about?" Dad asked, pointing at the book I had laid on the table before getting my cookies.

I finished chewing a bite of cookie. "There's this girl who goes out West to visit her cousins for the summer," I explained. "They give her a horse to ride, and it has a brand. She thinks the brand is weird because she's never seen one before."

"Pete had a brand you know," Dad said, dipping a cookie into his cup of coffee.

"Pete had brand?" I said.

"Sure did," Dad replied.

Pete and Ole, the last team of workhorses my father owned, had been gone from our farm for quite a few years by the time I was born. I didn't think Pete was such an unusual name for a horse, but Ole was a Norwegian name, and I could not figure out why the horse would have a Norwegian name. Mom was Norwegian. Dad was not. But my father had been the one who worked with the horses and fed them and took care of them, and it seemed unlikely to me that my mother would name the team. One time I had asked Mom how 'Ole' was spelled. Since it rhymed with 'holy' I thought it was probably 'O-l-y.' But Mom said no, that Ole was spelled 'O-l-e.'

"What did Pete's brand look like?" I asked.

I loved to watch Westerns on television. I knew that brands were markings burned into the hide of a horse or a cow with a hot iron so the ranch owners would know which animal belonged where if they got mixed up on the open range, and that when it came time to do the branding, every ranch hand had to pitch in and help—sort of like haying time on our farm where sometimes even my big sister became a tractor driver.

I was hoping the brand would be something interesting like a Circle Bar D, or a Double B, or a Triple R. The brands in the Westerns on television were like the name of the ranch. If the ranch was Circle Bar D Ranch, then the brand was a circle with a 'D' in the middle and a line over the 'D.'

"Pete's brand was nothing special," Dad replied. "Only a little squiggly mark on his hip."

"But Pete and Ole weren't really workhorses, were they?" I asked as I nibbled the edge off another oatmeal cookie. I knew all about the workhorse breeds from reading the H volume of our *World Book Encyclopedia* set. There were Clydesdales and Belgians and Percherons and Shires.

"Nope," Dad said. "Pete and Ole were just ordinary horses."

"What color were they?" I asked, although I already knew the answer to that question.

"They were brown," Loretta said.

"Yes, they were brown horses," said Mom, who had come out to the kitchen a minute ago.

"But what kind of brown?" I asked.

I knew horses could be many different colors of brown: sorrel (a reddish brown), chestnut (a darker brown), bay (reddish brown with a black mane and tail), roan (also a reddish brown but with white hairs mixed in), dun (yellowish brown with a dark brown stripe along the spine), and buckskin (a light brownish beige).

"I guess you could say they were sorrels," Dad replied.

"They still looked like plain old brown horses to me," Mom said.
"Would you like a cookie, Mother? And some coffee?" Loretta
asked.
"Yes, please," Mom replied.
My sister put a cookie on a small plate and poured a cup of coffee
for Mom.
I glanced at Dad. He was grinning.
"What's so funny, Daddy?" I asked.
"I was just thinking about Pete and Ole. Pete was thin and kind of
nervous. Ole was fat and slow. When I hooked them together, I had to
be careful about saying 'gid-up' and slapping the reins, because Pete
would take off like he'd been shot out of cannon."
"What would Ole do?" I asked.
"Not much," Dad replied. "Not any more than he had to. Ole didn't
want to move that fast. It didn't matter how many times I slapped the
reins, he'd hang back, and if we were plowing or something like that, it
meant Pete was doing most of the work. I think Ole figured he was just
out for a walk. Or to keep Pete company."
My mother took a sip of coffee and set the cup on the table. "I was
always surprised you ever got any work done with those two," she said.
I turned toward Dad again and nibbled some more off the edge of
my cookie. If it had been left up to me, I would have eaten half the
batch by myself this afternoon. But I knew Mom wouldn't like that,
and plus, if I ate so many cookies now, I wouldn't have enough during
the week while Loretta was at her apartment. Eating the cookies
reminded me that Loretta would come home again on the weekend. I
missed my big sister when she was gone.
"How did Pete and Ole get their names, anyway?" I asked.
"See, there were a lot of Norwegians around here back then," Dad
said. "Not like now, where people say they're Norwegian because of
their folks, but real Norwegians, people who came from the old
country."
Dad reached for his coffee cup. "They had this newspaper that was
written in Norwegian. I couldn't understand a word of it, but Nels
could."
Nels was my mother's father, and I knew he had died many years
before I was born.
"And in this newspaper," Dad continued, "they had a comic strip.
The characters' names were Pete and Ole. Nels would read it and

laugh, and so would Sigurd if he happened to be over here. And then I'd ask what was so funny, and they'd tell me what Pete and Ole were doing that week."

Sigurd was Mom's uncle.

"Did you like Grandpa Nels, Daddy? And Uncle Sigurd? Were they nice?"

I could remember Uncle Sigurd. He had died when I was five years old. He had lived in town, and I would go with Loretta to bring him out to the farm to eat Sunday dinner with us.

"Yeah," Dad said, "Nels and I got along fine. Same with Sigurd. They were both nice guys. I used to cut pulp with Sigurd. When Ma got polio, Nels helped me take care of your brother and sister."

"But what about the comic strip, Dad?"

"The characters were always getting themselves into one situation or another, and so, when we got this team of horses, I thought it sounded like good names for them. Turned out to be accurate, too, because Pete and Ole were always doing funny things."

Dad went to the stove to fill his cup and came back to the table with another handful of cookies. If it was one thing Dad liked, it was sweets, but he said he couldn't understand it because the Norwegians were the ones who were supposed to like sweets, and his father came from Scotland and his mother came from Germany. He figured that liking sweets must mean lots of Norwegian had rubbed off on him, seeing as he had lived around them for so long.

"What else do you remember about Pete and Ole?" I asked.

Dad dipped another cookie into his coffee. "When I worked at the canning factory," he said, "I didn't have time during the week to fool with the horses."

For as long as I had known my father, he had been a farmer, and I had a hard time picturing him at work in a factory.

"Why were you working at the canning factory?"

"We needed the money," Mom said.

"But what about Pete and Ole?" I asked.

"All week long while I was at the factory, they'd stand around, eating. Getting fat. Doing nothing. When I was home, I'd walk out to the pasture to see 'em. And there they'd be. All over me. Nuzzling my arm. Nudging my cap. Following me around like big puppy dogs."

He reached for another cookie.

"Although," Dad continued, "it was a different story entirely if I wanted to get some work done."

"Then what happened?"

"They'd take one look at me—and they'd run!" Dad recalled. "Tails in the air. Kicking up clods of dirt. They'd gallop around and around the pasture. You'd think they were race horses instead of workhorses."

My sister pulled another cookie sheet out of the oven. "I remember that," she said. "Especially the part about them kicking up big hunks of dirt when they ran away."

"How'd you ever catch them?" I asked.

"Oh—once they got it out of their system, they'd settle down," Dad said. "Then they'd let me catch them just as nice as you please."

My father rubbed his ear. "You know, sometimes I thought it seemed like Pete and Ole missed me when I was gone all week."

"Then why did they run away?"

"That's a horse for you," Mom said. "You can't get a hold of them when you want them."

"Horses are smart that way," Dad said. "They know the difference between when you want to catch 'em for work and when you're only coming out there to see them."

"Pete and Ole must not have liked working," I said.

"Actually," Dad said. "I don't think Pete and Ole minded working. Everybody likes to feel useful, you know. It's just that it was a trick they enjoyed playing."

"Sort of like a game?"

"*Exactly* like a game," Dad replied.

He picked up his coffee cup, saw that it was empty, and stood up.

"And then, too, there was that time Loretta and Ingman took Pete and Ole for a ride," he said, as he headed for the coffee pot.

"You want some more coffee, Ma?" he asked.

My mother held up her hand, as if to say 'no,' but then thought better of it. "Maybe a half a cup," she said.

I turned toward Loretta. "How come you were riding the horses? Were you going out to get the cows?"

My sister ran water into the cookie batter bowl. "I don't remember why we decided to take Pete and Ole out for a ride," she said. "Ingman rode Pete because he liked to go fast. I liked Ole because he was slow."

"What happened?" I asked.

"When we came to a tree, Ole was much too lazy to go around, so he walked right under it," Loretta said.

"Then what?" I asked.

"A tree branch knocked me off," Loretta said as she started to put the cooled cookies into a canister.

"How come you didn't duck?"

"Duck?" Loretta asked, turning to stare at me. "I was too scared to think about ducking."

"Why were you scared?"

"Ole was a big animal."

"Did he run away after you fell off?"

"Oh, no. He just stopped and stood there."

"How come you didn't turn him away from the tree?"

"Me? Try to turn that great big thing?" Loretta asked, looking horrified at the very thought.

Turning was easy. You pulled on the rein in the direction you wanted to go. That's what I did with Dusty.

"Wasn't it fun to ride the horses?" I asked.

If Pete and Ole were still here, I knew I would want to ride them every day. When it came to the workhorses, I was jealous of Loretta and Ingman because they had known Pete and Ole personally.

Loretta turned toward me and shook her finger. "I've never ridden a horse since then," she declared, "and I haven't wanted to, either!"

Dad sat back in his chair and crossed one leg over the other. "And then there was the time Pete and Ole came home all by themselves," he said. "Some people we know wanted to use them during the week while I was gone at work. Pete and Ole came home, in the middle of the night, all by themselves."

"By *themselves*?" I said.

"But nobody knew it," Mom said, "not until Loretta and Ingman came home from school the next day."

"Why not?" I said.

"Because they stayed behind the barn, where I couldn't see them," Mom said.

"When Ingman and I were on our way back from school and got over the hill, we could see them behind the barn," Loretta explained. "We hurried the rest of the way home because we wanted to know why Pete and Ole were back so soon."

My mother shook her head. "When they came in the house and said Pete and Ole were behind the barn, I thought they were seeing things."

"I guess Pete and Ole didn't want to be someplace else," Dad said. "They wanted to come home. They traveled quite a few miles to get here, too."

He sighed, and a far-away look came into his blue eyes. "Yup—Pete and Ole were quite the pair..."

"What happened to them?" I asked.

"I sold them," Mom said.

"You what?"

"Sold them. While your father was away at work."

"Why?" I said.

"Oh, it wasn't as bad as it sounds," Dad said. "By that time we had a tractor, and we really didn't need the horses anymore."

"But your father couldn't stand to see them leave. So, I told the guy he had to take them before my husband came home from work," Mom said.

A lump rose in my throat. I knew how I would feel if I came home from school one day and found out Dusty was gone.

"What happened to Pete and Ole after that?" I asked.

"Don't know," Dad said. "Didn't see nor hear anything of 'em. It was so long ago now, I'm sure they're both dead."

Later that evening while we were doing the chores, in between carrying milk to the milkhouse for Dad, I got Dusty out of her stall and tied her in the barn aisle so I could brush her.

"Well, Dusty, are you enjoying getting brushed?" Dad asked.

He had finished putting a milker on a cow and had come over to see my pony. At the sound of his voice, Dusty turned her head toward him.

"You're a good girl, aren't you," Dad said as he rubbed her forehead.

Dusty's forelock had not grown back much yet after her haircut last fall when it was full of cockleburs. Instead of a thick, white foretop hanging down between her eyes, it was a clump of bushy white hair sticking up between her ears.

Dad stopped scratching Dusty's forehead, and she pushed her nose under his arm and nudged him hard enough to make his arm bounce up and down.

Dad laughed and patted her neck. "You're as bad as Pete and Ole. Do you know that?"

"Daddy?"

"What, kiddo."

"Do you wish Mom hadn't sold Pete and Ole?"

Dad didn't say anything for so long that I thought he wasn't going to answer my question. Instead he stroked Dusty's velvety brown nose with one calloused hand. When he turned to look at me, my father's blue eyes had lost their usual twinkle.

"I would have liked to keep Pete and Ole forever," he said. "They were my friends."

Before I could think of another question to ask, he turned and walked back to the cow so he could check on the milker.

I put my arms around Dusty's neck and buried my face in her thick hair. Dusty's reddish brown winter coat felt as soft as the fur trimming on the winter boots my sister wore when she was dressed up for work or for church. Dusty's dapples, I had noticed, were not nearly as easy to see during the winter when her hair was longer. I took a deep breath and held it. If I lived to be four hundred years old, I would never grow tired of the smell of horses.

"Smells good, don't she," Dad said.

I looked up and saw that he was taking the cover off a full bucket of milk.

"Daddy, I'm sorry you didn't get to keep Pete and Ole."

Dad put the cover on an empty milker bucket. "It's all right, kiddo," he said. "That was years ago. Water under the bridge, as they say."

My father's words *said* it was all right, but I could tell by the way he said it that it was not—not really.

And even though I knew Pete and Ole had both probably died years ago, I couldn't help wishing they were still alive so I could find them and bring them home again.

****

~ 17 ~
The Day After Valentine's

One afternoon I hung up my school coat in the hall closet and decided once and for all to ask a question that had been bothering me for a quite a while. My mother was in the living room, sitting in her chair by the picture window, and we were the only two people in the house. The aroma of a freshly-baked chocolate cake lingered in the air, and I saw that Mom had set the cake on the cutting board to cool. I hardly gave the cake a second glance, though, as I went into the living room.

"Mom? How come you and Dad didn't get married on Valentine's Day?"

Mom and Dad's wedding anniversary was February 15.

My mother shifted her attention away from a magazine she was reading. "What would make you ask that?" she wondered.

"We're getting ready for Valentine's Day at school, and that made me start thinking about it," I said.

"Well," she said, "we just didn't, that's all."

"But how come?" I persisted.

I sat on the floor by my mother's chair and pulled my skirt down over my knees. This morning I had put on my favorite red sweater, a plaid skirt and white cable-knit knee-socks. I owned a couple of pairs of leotards, but when the weather was not below zero—which it hadn't been for at least a week—I would rather wear knee-socks than leotards. Girls were allowed to wear pants to school only on Fridays.

"Let's see..." Mom said, "I guess I don't remember why we picked the fifteenth. That was a long time ago. More than thirty years."

"You don't *remember*?" I said.

Mom frowned as she searched back in her memory. "We were married on a Monday..."

Monday? The weddings at our church often were on Saturday, although once or twice weddings had taken place on Sunday afternoon, too.

"Why did you pick Monday? Sunday would have been Valentine's Day," I pointed out.

"Things were different back then," she said. "We didn't pay much attention to Valentine's Day."

I, quite frankly, could not even begin to imagine such a thing. For the past week, since the beginning of February, we had been busy at school getting ready for Valentine's, decorating our mailboxes, talking about what we were going to wear for our Valentine's Day party, and cutting out pink and red and white hearts to decorate the windows and the bulletin boards and the door. Or rather, the girls were busy talking about what we were going to wear to the party and making pink and red and white hearts. The boys didn't seem too interested in what they were going to wear *or* in decorating our room for Valentine's.

"But why didn't you pay much attention to Valentine's Day?" I asked.

My mother sighed, a sound that fell somewhere between exasperated and resigned. She leaned back in the chair and folded her hands. "During the '30s, times were hard. We didn't have much money."

"Was that because of the Depression?"

"Yes," she said.

I had heard Mom talk about the Great Depression before and how people would put newspaper in their shoes to cover up holes in the bottom—and that instead of buying new dresses, or buying material to make new dresses, women would take the collars and cuffs and hems apart and would sew them again so the worn spots wouldn't show—and that people could buy a brand new shirt for twenty-five cents, except that no one *had* twenty-five cents.

In the little copper tea canister sitting on the kitchen cupboard, which my mother said I could use for my 'valuables' because she never stored tea in it anyway, I had saved a small collection of quarters, dimes, nickels and pennies. Sometimes Mom would pay me fifty cents for doing a cleaning job during my summer vacation from school that she could not do herself and which she did not think Loretta should have to do on the weekend, such as taking everything out of the storage space underneath the steps that we called the pantry, scrubbing the wooden floor and walls with Pine-Sol, and then putting everything back where it belonged. A couple of times I had also washed the concrete porch floor. Mom could scrub the kitchen floor, but she said the porch floor was too hard on her knees. And once, I had scrubbed the concrete basement floor. While Mom stood in the doorway and supervised, I had used one of the push brooms from the barn to scrub the floor, and after I was finished, I had used an old wringer mop to sop up the dirty water.

Whenever Mom counted out the change as my payment for the cleaning jobs, she would tell me to save my money so the next time I wanted candy or gum or another horse magazine, I could buy it for myself. The idea that a quarter could buy candy or gum if I wanted it was one thing, but I could hardly imagine what it would be like if a new shirt cost twenty-five cents, and I really needed a new shirt because my old one was worn out and full of holes, but I didn't have twenty-five cents to buy a shirt.

With my arms wrapped around my knees, I began to rock back and forth. Even if I was not sitting in the rocking chair, the motion of rocking helped me to think.

"Is that why you and Dad don't have wedding rings?" I asked. "Because you didn't have any money to buy them?"

Mom brushed the magazine cover with the tips of her fingers. "Yes, that's right. We couldn't afford them."

At the houses of several of my friends, I had seen their parents' wedding pictures. The brides held big bouquets of pretty flowers and wore long, white wedding gowns decorated with yards of lace.

I unwrapped my arms from around my knees. "Is that why you and Dad don't have any wedding pictures? Because you couldn't afford it?"

Once again, my mother nodded.

Several girls at school had weddings coming up soon in their families. One girl's sister was getting married, and another girl's cousin was getting married, and just about every opportunity that came along, they talked about the wedding dresses, and the bridesmaids dresses, and the flowers, and the wedding cake, and how the church was going to be decorated, and what their mothers were going to wear, and what *they* were going to wear. One of the girls was even going to be something called a junior bridesmaid, and she said she was supposed to wear a long dress, would carry flowers, and that her aunt had said they couldn't have a wedding without a junior bridesmaid.

I leaned back on my hands. "Did you have a wedding dress, Mom? I mean, a real one?"

My mother shook her head.

"What did you wear?"

"Oh," she replied, "it was an ordinary dress. My best dress that I wore to church."

"Did you have any flowers?"

"No, no flowers," Mom said.

"Bridesmaids?" I asked, although I was fairly certain I already knew the answer.

"Nope," Mom replied. "Just Reuben and Gertie as our witnesses."

Reuben, of course, was Mom's cousin. Gertie was his wife.

"Where did you get married?"

I was sure that she would say they had gotten married at the little white country church a half mile from our farm. My mother's parents and aunts and uncles had helped start the church way back in the old days when people still used horses for transportation. And I knew Mom had been going to church there since she was a little girl.

"We got married at the parsonage," my mother replied.

The parsonage was a large, white house in town. The bottom part of the front porch was built of real fieldstone. And from the upstairs window, my mother said that other people had told her you could see the river winding its way south.

"Not the parsonage we have now," Mom added quickly. "It was a different one. The three churches didn't buy this house until a few years before you were born."

The church south of our farm was one of three churches in the parish all served by the same minister.

I leaned back on my hands. "Which house was the parsonage, then?"

"It was one of the other houses in town," Mom replied.

"How old were you when you got married?" I asked.

"I was twenty," Mom said.

"And you were twenty-six when you got polio, and you were forty-two when I was born, right?" I said.

"Right," she replied.

Suddenly I began to feel very sad. No Valentine's Day wedding. No special dress. No flowers, no bridesmaids, no pictures. Not even any wedding rings.

"That was all a very long time ago," Mom said. "It's funny, though—to think back to how desperately poor we were then."

I knew very little about the current state of my parents' finances, but I was pretty sure they were not 'desperately poor.'

And then, all at once, a wonderful idea popped into my head.

"I know—you and Daddy could buy wedding rings NOW!" I pointed out gleefully, sitting bolt upright.

Mom's eyes widened with surprise. "Buy wedding rings? Now? What for?"

"So you could wear them…I mean, lots of other people wear wedding rings…other moms and dads…and my teachers at school…"

My mother laughed and reached out to touch my hair. "Sweetheart," she said, "we don't need wedding rings."

"You don't?"

"Of course not. We're just as married without them. It isn't wedding rings that makes you married. Or pictures or dresses or flowers, for that matter."

I wrapped my arms around my knees again. "Then what *does* make you married?"

"The ceremony itself. That's what's important. The vows you take," she said.

I knew that 'vow' is another word for 'promise' but that a vow is more important than a promise, a vow is *stronger* than a promise. All my life, Mom had been telling me that I should never promise to do something if I did not intend to do it, and that it was better not to promise to do something than to promise but not do it. The way Mom talked about promises, and keeping promises, and breaking promises, for a long time, I hadn't realized there was anything stronger than a promise.

"You've been to a couple of weddings," Mom said. "Do you remember what they said?"

I considered her question. "You mean when they say, 'For better, for worse?'"

"Yes," she said. "The vows also say 'For richer, for poorer, in sickness and in health.'"

"And after you say that, you're married?" I asked.

"Yes—if you say it in front of a minister—because you have promised—vowed—to stay with that person through everything," Mom explained.

"But what about the dresses and the flowers and the rings?"

"Those are nice to have, but they are not *necessary*," Mom said. "Do you see what I mean?"

I stretched out my legs and refolded the top of one sock and then the other one.

"I *think* I know what you mean," I said when the tops of my knee socks were adjusted just so.

"Tell me what you think I mean," Mom replied.

"I think you mean," I said slowly, "that it doesn't matter what you wear or if you carry flowers or if you have rings because you can say the vows without any of those."

"Yes," Mom said.

"But if you wear a wedding dress and have flowers and rings, but you don't say the vows, then you're not married," I continued.

"Well, yes, I guess that's right, too," she said.

I stood up and brushed off the back of my skirt. The skirt was made of wool, but it was lined with satin.

"Are you sure you and Daddy shouldn't buy wedding rings?" I asked.

"I'm sure," Mom said. She smiled. "I don't think Dad would wear one, anyway. He'd probably rather put the money toward—oh, I don't know—a new fishing pole."

I paused in thought. "Or parts for the manure spreader."

Now it was Mom's turn to think.

"Or a portable air compressor. He's been talking about how an air compressor would come in handy," she said.

"But Mom," I said, "what would *you* put the money toward?"

My mother frowned. "I don't know. I think I have everything I need. We've got plenty to eat. The house is warm. And we all have clothes to wear that are not worn out."

"But there must be *something* you'd like," I said.

She hesitated and stared out the window at the yard, as if she were searching for something.

"If there was only one thing I could have," she said at last, turning toward me, "I would like to be able to go for a walk around the farm again. Just once. But all of the money in the world can't buy that."

My mother laid the magazine on the floor next to her chair and reached for her crutches. "Say—there's cake out in the kitchen, you know. I'll make some frosting, and then let's have a piece of cake."

We went to the kitchen, and as my mother measured powdered sugar to make frosting, it occurred to me that I had not asked whether they'd had a wedding cake, although I was pretty sure I knew the answer.

I also still did not truly know why they had gotten married the day after Valentine's. Except that while I watched Mom stir the frosting, I thought maybe I did know, after all, because if the flowers, the dress and the rings were not important, then the day itself—whether it was the fourteenth or the fifteenth—was not important.

What an afternoon this had been. I started out asking one question, ended up asking many more questions, and discovered some surprising answers. I could hardly wait to tell the girls at school they didn't need any of those things for weddings that they spent so much time talking about.

On second thought, maybe I shouldn't tell them. They would probably never believe me, anyhow.

Especially not the girl who was going to be a junior bridesmaid.

****

~ 18 ~
Gertrude and Heathcliff

I settled into the bus seat next to the window, and my best friend, Vicki, flopped down in the seat next to the aisle. Seeing as Vicki got off the bus before I did, although only a little while before I did, it made more sense for her to sit on the outside rather than on the inside by the window. A light snow had begun to fall earlier in the afternoon, and a few minutes later, as the bus pulled out from in front of the school, I hoped that it would snow hard enough for a day off from school tomorrow. So far, we'd only had one snow day, and I could hardly wait for another one.

Vicki and I had been best friends for nearly two years, practically ever since she and her family had moved to the area, but it still seemed unbelievable to me: a girl from my grade, who was my best friend, who rode the same bus as me, and *who only lived a short way from our farm.* I'd never had anyone the same age as me live so close. The next-closest girl from my class lived five miles away.

The farm where Vicki lived was not a dairy farm, it was a turkey farm, and it was not owned by her family, it was owned by a company, but the most important thing was that she lived only a mile and a half away. During the summer, we rode our bikes back and forth between houses, and during the winter, on weekends sometimes, Vicki's dad would bring her to my house, or Loretta would take me to Vicki's house. Vicki helped me with my chores in the barn, and during the summer, when the turkeys were outside in the fields, I helped Vicki with her chores. I liked going to Vicki's house because—

"Guess what?" Vicki said, interrupting my thoughts.

I turned to look at her.

"What?" I said.

"I forgot to tell you this before!" she said. "We're going to visit our relatives down south next weekend!"

'Down south' meant the southern part of the state, I knew, not Alabama or Florida or Louisiana.

"How come?" I said.

Vicki unzipped her coat and stuffed her stocking cap into one of the pockets. The heater was going full blast, and it was starting to feel warm in the bus.

"We're going just because, I guess. Mom and Dad want to visit before we get more turkeys this spring. After that, we won't have time," she said.

It was, I thought, the same reason Dad went sucker fishing in the spring. My father liked to go sucker fishing before he started plowing and planting because after he started the field work, he wouldn't have much time to go fishing.

"And Mom said I'm supposed to ask you if you would take care of Gertrude and Heathcliff while we're gone," Vicki added. "We could bring them to your house. You wouldn't have to come over to my house to take care of them."

I gazed at Vicki, wide-eyed. "Do you mean it? I could take care of Gertrude and Heathcliff?"

Not long after Vicki and I became friends, Vicki's family had acquired two parakeets. One was blue and the other was yellow. And their names were Gertrude and Heathcliff. I had always thought it might be fun to have a bird, and after getting to know Gertrude and Heathcliff, I was *sure* it would be fun.

My mother, unfortunately, wanted no part of it.

"Birds," she had declared when I brought up the subject, "are noisy and smelly. Besides, I've heard they're hard to keep. A month or two at the most before something happens to them, and you wouldn't want to get attached to a bird and then have it die right away, would you?"

I had to agree with my mother. I would not want the bird to die soon after I got it. But as for her other claims, that birds were noisy and smelly, well, I had been in Vicki's house many times and Gertrude and Heathcliff were not at all noisy. And they were not smelly. Compared to even one pair of the barn boots that sat in our porch, Gertrude and Heathcliff were as stinky as lilacs or roses or peonies.

"And you know what else?" Vicki said. "Maybe if Gertrude and Heathcliff stay with you for the weekend, your mom will see they're nice and then she'll let you get a bird."

I had been thinking the same thing, but as soon as the words were out of Vicki's mouth, I knew it would never work. Mom had said in no uncertain terms that she did not want a bird in her house. Ever. Period. End of discussion.

"That won't work," I said.

"It might," Vicki replied.

I shook my head. "Mom probably won't even let me take care of Gertrude and Heathcliff."

"Why not?"

"Because she said she did not want a bird in her house. Ever. Period. End of discussion," I said.

"Yikes," Vicki said.

As the countryside slipped past the bus windows, Vicki and I remained quiet, each lost in our own thoughts. The snow was falling faster in tiny flakes, driven by a strong wind that I knew would sting my face when I walked up the hill from the bus. It was snowing hard enough to make it difficult to see very far in the distance, and if the snow continued this way, maybe we wouldn't have school tomorrow.

"Well," Vicki said at last, "could you ask, anyway, to see if your mom might let you take care of Gertrude and Heathcliff?"

"Oh, sure," I said, "I can ask. But I don't think she will let me do it."

"Just ask," Vicki said. "My mom said she would feel better if Gertrude and Heathcliff were at your house because you've helped me clean their cage and feed them and water them, and you know what to do to take care of them."

For the remainder of the route, until it was time for Vicki to get off the bus, we talked about other things: the story we were reading in class, a social studies project that was due in a few days, the best way to go tobogganing the next time Vicki was able to come to my house (whether we should ride together or take turns going down the hill).

We had not yet made a decision about tobogganing when the bus stopped in front of Vicki's driveway. Even though they only lived a mile and a half away, their farm—which was one whole section, which meant that it was one mile square, or in other words, was 640 acres, as Dad explained it—was as flat as could be. That was one of the reasons Vicki liked coming to my house. Our farm had hills and plenty of good places to go tobogganing.

Not long after Vicki got off the bus, the driver turned down our road. The bus crested first one hill and then the next and then the bus driver was downshifting so he could turn into our driveway. No one else got off the bus farther up on our road, so the driver always turned around in our driveway and headed back out to the highway.

I jumped down the last step off the bus, stood with my books clasped between my knees and reached back to pull up the hood of my coat. Behind me, the bus doors clattered shut, and I heard the driver shift into reverse. When I finished tying my hood, the bus had already backed out of the driveway, and soon we were headed in opposite directions—me going up the hill toward the house and the bus going out toward the main road.

The snow did not sting my face nearly so much with my hood over my head, although I also noticed it was not snowing as hard as it had been a little while ago. For once, instead of hurrying up the hill, I took my time. I kept hoping that if I walked slowly enough, I would think of a good way to ask Mom if I could take care of Gertrude and Heathcliff.

Needles came from the direction of the granary after I reached the top of the hill. His tail was going in circles, and I stopped and petted him. He looked up at me with his round, brown eyes, and his whole body wiggled when his tail wagged. I gave Needles one final pat, went into the porch, took off my boots, walked into the kitchen, took my coat off, hung it over the back of Dad's chair and pulled the chair closer to the furnace grate. My coat was covered with snow, and I knew that if it wasn't dry before I stowed it away in the closet, it might be damp in the morning when I put it on again.

I still didn't know what I was going to say about Gertrude and Heathcliff.

"Snowing kind of hard out there, isn't it," Mom said. "It's not supposed to snow much, though, only a few inches." She was sitting by the table with the newspaper that came every day open in front of her. Next to the newspaper an apple core occupied the center of a small plate, so I knew that Mom had recently been eating an apple and reading the newspaper.

"I've got a present for Dusty," Mom said, gesturing toward the apple core.

Mom saved her apple cores for Dusty and so did Dad and Loretta, although Ingman sometimes forgot and threw them away. I saved my apple cores for Dusty, too, except if I was eating an apple when I went out to see her, then more often than not, I gave her half of my apple.

"Mom?" I said.

"Hmmmmm?" my mother replied as she turned to the next the page of the newspaper.

"I know you don't like birds," I began, "but...well...Vicki and her family are going away for a few days...next weekend actually...to visit relatives...and..."

Mom looked up from the newspaper. "And what?" she asked, her eyes narrowing.

"Well...ahhh...she wants to know if we could...ahhhhh...take care of Gertrude and Heathcliff while they're gone."

If there was one thing I could count on about my mother, it was that I knew she would not keep me in suspense when I asked a question like that.

"No. Absolutely not. I don't want the responsibility," she said.

"Mo-om, you didn't even *think* about it!" I replied.

She shook her head.

"But Mom, it's only for a few days."

"I don't care if it's only for a few hours. We're not taking care of those birds," she said.

"Why not?" I said. "You won't have to do anything with them. I will clean the cage and give them food and water. Please? Gertrude and Heathcliff won't be any trouble. You'll see."

"And what if one of them dies while they're here?" Mom replied. "No, I do not want to take the responsibility."

I drew a deep breath. "Mooo-ther. Nothing is going to happen to Gertrude and Heathcliff. Nothing's happened to them so far, has it? They've had Gertrude and Heathcliff for a long time. Since last year."

"I still don't think it's a very good idea," she said.

"Please? Please-please-please? They're not noisy or smelly...or anything..."

Mom gazed at me steadily without blinking.

"If we don't take care of Gertrude and Heathcliff, what will they do with them for the weekend?" she asked.

"I don't know," I said. "Vicki said that her mom said she would like Gertrude and Heathcliff to stay here because I've helped Vicki clean their cage and give them food and water so I know what to do to take care of them."

My mother drummed her fingers against the top of the table as she considered whether Gertrude and Heathcliff could stay with us for the weekend.

"Oh, all right," she said at last. "I suppose it wouldn't hurt just this once. But if anything happens..."

I could feel a grin stretching across my face. "Nothing will happen. You won't even know they're here."

As it turned out, Vicki's mom and dad decided to leave on Friday, so the following Thursday evening before supper, Vicki and her dad brought Gertrude and Heathcliff to our house.

"We'll be back Sunday afternoon, and we'll come over to get them then if that's all right," Vicki's dad said.

"Oh, sure, that's fine," Mom replied. She leaned forward to get a closer look at Gertrude and Heathcliff. The cage sat on the table next to my mother. The two birds huddled side by side on their wide perch swing, looking back at Mom.

"You're pretty little birds, aren't you," she said. "Very pretty little birds."

My mother was not the kind of person who talked to animals, except maybe to tell Needles, or the barn cats who liked to sit on the porch steps, that they were in her way and that they would have to move so she wouldn't fall over them.

"Where would you like me to set up the stand ?" Vicki's dad asked.

Gertrude and Heathcliff's cage normally hung suspended from a stand made especially for that purpose.

Mom pulled her gaze away from Gertrude and Heathcliff. "Oh, you can set that up anywhere in the living room," she said.

Vicki's dad set up the stand, and Vicki carried Gertrude and Heathcliff's cage into the living room and hung it from the hook.

"Oh, yes, I almost forgot," Vicki's dad said, pulling a small paper bag out of his pocket. "Here's their birdseed. And at night, put a towel over their cage. They go to sleep when there's a towel over them."

I took the paper bag and set it on the floor beneath the cage.

"Okay, Gertrude and Heathcliff," Vicki said, looking in at the two birds sitting side by side, "you'll be here for a few days, but we'll come and get you on Sunday."

"Be good birdies," Vicki's dad added.

A few minutes later, Vicki and her father left, and a little while after that, Dad came in the house for supper. He washed his hands and then went into the living room to watch the news.

"I see our company has arrived," Dad said, peering into the cage at Gertrude and Heathcliff. The two birds were still sitting on their perch.

"What's the matter with them, Daddy?" I asked.

"Why? What do you mean?" Dad said.

"They haven't moved off their perch since they got here. And they haven't made any kind of sound," I said.

"How would you feel if someone took you to a place you'd never been before and then left you by yourself with people you didn't know?" Dad said.

I looked at Gertrude and Heathcliff. "Do you think they're scared, Daddy?"

He shook his head. "Not scared, exactly, but maybe not too sure of themselves yet."

During supper, Gertrude and Heathcliff remained quiet, although by the time we came in the house after doing the evening milking, the parakeets were hopping around their cage, eating birdseed, drinking water, and twittering and squeaking and chattering.

"You woke up, I see," Dad said to the birds as he peered into their cage. He turned and sat down on the davenport.

"Oh, my, yes, did they ever," Mom replied. "And they've been very good company, too."

I looked at Dad—and he looked at me. Then we both looked at Mom.

"What are you two looking at me like that for?" my mother asked.

Dad leaned forward and reached around behind him to adjust the pillow that cushioned his lower back.

"I thought you didn't like birds," he said.

"Well, I don't. Not as a general rule," Mom replied. "But Gertrude and Heathcliff are awfully cute. And they were good company while you were out in the barn."

"I see," Dad said. He pressed his lips together in such a way that meant he was trying not to smile.

When we were ready to go to bed, I fetched a towel from the bathroom and put it over Gertrude and Heathcliff's cage, and the next morning, I got up fifteen minutes early so I would have time to clean their cage and give them more birdseed and fresh water. An hour and a half later, after I had been out in the barn and was upstairs getting dressed for school, I heard Mom talking to Gertrude and Heathcliff, once again telling them they were pretty birds and that they were good company.

Almost before I realized how fast the time was going, it was Sunday afternoon, and Vicki and her dad had arrived to pick up Gertrude and Heathcliff.

"Were you good birdies?" Vicki's dad asked.

"They were extremely good birds," my mother said. She put her hands on the arms of her chair and pushed herself to a standing position, leaned down, picked up her crutches, and then made her way over to Gertrude and Heathcliff's cage.

"Thank you for bringing them to stay," she said. "I didn't realize it would be so much fun to have birds in the house."

"They are fun to have around," Vicki's dad said. "I'm glad everything worked out so well."

Vicki's father wrapped a blanket around the cage. The two of them turned and headed out through the porch, and I walked to the car with them.

"See?" Vicki said. "I *told* you it would work. Your mother liked them, so now maybe you can get a bird, too."

"Yeah!" I said. "Maybe!"

Not long after Vicki and her dad disappeared down the driveway, Mom mentioned how quiet the house seemed without Gertrude and Heathcliff. She said it again during supper, and yet again soon after I came in from the barn, and it was then that I decided to bring up the subject.

"Mom? I know you don't like birds, but Gertrude and Heathcliff are so nice, and well, could we *maybe* get a bird?"

My mother brushed back one lock of curly dark hair that had fallen across her forehead. "Gertrude and Heathcliff really are cute, aren't they." She paused. "Let me think about it for a while. Would that be all right?"

"Okay," I said, although the truth of the matter is that it was much more than 'okay' because I was pretty sure Mom would say, 'yes.'

"And here you were so afraid something would happen to them while they were here," I said.

Mom smiled. "Yes, I suppose I worried about it too much, didn't I."

The next morning, I waited impatiently for the bus to arrive. I could hardly wait to tell Vicki that we were going to get a bird, or rather, that I was almost certain we were going to get a bird. Since last night, I had been busy thinking about names, and I wanted Vicki to help me pick the right one.

The bus driver was not driving any slower than he did on other days, but this morning, the route to Vicki's house seemed to be taking an exceptionally long time. Eventually the bus stopped by Vicki's driveway, and I waited anxiously for the bus driver to open the door and for Vicki to climb the steps.

"Guess what?" I said as she flopped into the seat beside me. "Guess wh—"

I took a closer look at my friend. Her eyes were red, and she was sniffling.

"What's the matter?" I asked.

"It's Heathcliff," she said.

"What about him?"

"He…ahhh…he…died."

"*What*?

"He's dead."

"Are you sure?"

Vicki took off her stocking cap and laid it in her lap. "We found him upside-down in his cage this morning."

I stared at her, not quite knowing what to say.

Cute, perky, adorable little Heathcliff? *Dead*?

And then I had a dreadful thought.

"Didn't I take good enough care of him?" I asked.

Vicki reached into her coat pocket for a tissue and blew her nose. "Mom and Dad said they thought maybe it was too much in and out of the cold for him, going back and forth between houses. But Mom also said it might have happened anyway, even if we hadn't gone away this weekend."

"Oh," I said.

As soon as I got home from school in the afternoon, I was faced with the unpleasant job of telling Mom that Heathcliff had died.

"He *died*?" she said. "Oh, no. Oh, the poor little thing…"

My mother reached into the pocket of her dress, pulled out a white handkerchief with pink crocheting around the edge and dabbed at her eyes.

"I hope it wasn't something we did—or that we didn't do," she said, slipping the handkerchief back into her pocket.

"Vicki said her mom and dad thought maybe going out into the cold was too much for him," I said. "Or Vicki's mom said it might have happened, anyway, even if they didn't go away for a few days."

My mother shook her head. "I've always heard that birds are hard to keep. I'm glad he didn't die while he was here. I wouldn't have wanted to be the one to tell them their bird had died when they came over here to get them."

Now that she mentioned it, I wouldn't have wanted to tell them, either.

I had been right about one thing, though: nothing had happened to Gertrude and Heathcliff while they were at our house.

On the other hand, maybe my mother had a point about birds, after all...

＊＊＊＊＊＊＊＊＊＊＊＊＊＊＊＊＊＊＊＊＊＊＊＊＊＊＊＊

~19 ~
Nothin' Like Homemade

The teacher turned the lights off, and I settled back in my chair to watch the movie. We rarely watched movies at school, maybe once a month, or every other month, and seeing as this movie was about making maple syrup, I wanted to make sure I paid close attention. Sometimes when we ate breakfast at home, Dad would talk about when he was a little boy and had stayed at the lumber camp in northern Wisconsin where his parents were cooks. They often ate pancakes and maple syrup for breakfast at the lumber camp, he said, and it was just about the best thing he had ever eaten.

I had never tasted maple syrup myself. Mom said it was too expensive. I asked Dad what maple syrup tasted like, and he had thought about it for a while and then said it reminded him of the way a freshly cut maple tree smells. "And it's sweet," he had added. "Much sweeter than any other syrup."

I'd never been around any freshly cut maple trees, but a couple of times during summer thunderstorms, branches had broken off the maple trees in the yard, so I knew what he was talking about concerning the smell of freshly cut maple. Pancakes also happened to be my favorite breakfast, especially when Dad made pancakes, although Mom's pancakes were good, too, it's just that Dad seemed to have so much fun making them. But whether it was Mom's pancakes or Dad's pancakes, either way, it seemed to me that pancakes with maple syrup would be a heavenly combination.

At the back of the room, the movie projector clicked and whirred as the film wound its way through the machine and back onto the other reel and then the screen was filled with a snowy woods and tree trunks with pegs sticking out of them and pails hung on the pegs. The first step in making maple syrup, the narrator said, was collecting sap from the maple trees, which could only be done at a special time of the year. The sap, he said, started to go up into the trees in March. The trees were called sugar maples, and their sap was especially good for making maple syrup, although the sap from all maple trees was sweet. Putting the pegs in the trunks was called 'tapping' the trees, and…

Suddenly, I could not focus on what the guy in the movie was saying because of something he had just said. What was it? Something to do with the trees and the sap. He had said…"the sap from all maple trees is sweet."

All maple trees.

I had no idea how many different maple trees there were, but I knew where to find one kind of maple tree. We had maple trees growing in our yard. They were called silver maples. And the trees were big. As big as the trees in the movie.

And something else the guy said had caught my attention, too: he said the sap starts to run in March. Not February, which was last month. And not April, which was next month. But March, the month that it was right now.

I sat back, feeling like I was in a dream.

If it was March—and we had maple trees—then could we make maple syrup at home?

I sat up straight again. I wanted to listen to the rest of the movie so I would know how to make maple syrup, although as the movie projector continued to click and whir, and the film wound its way through the machine, I learned that making maple syrup merely involved cooking the sap until it was thick. Mom made pancake syrup from brown sugar, water and butter and boiled the mixture until it was thick. And wouldn't that be the same process? I was pretty sure that it *was*.

When the movie ended, the teacher turned on the lights in our classroom, and I saw by the black-and-white clock above the door that we had an hour of school left. One whole hour. How was I ever going to make it through an entire hour?

I somehow managed to get through the next hour and through the bus ride home. Before the bus driver could even start backing out of the driveway, I was hurrying up the hill. A thick layer of gray clouds which looked like dirty cottonballs covered the sky, but even though the air felt damp and chilly, a thin trickle of water ran down the side of the driveway next to the snowbanks. As I trotted around the curve at the top of the driveway, it seemed to me the snowbanks were not as high as they had been a few days ago, but maybe that was only my imagination.

I stopped in the porch to kick off my winter boots, and when I pushed open the door leading into the kitchen, I could hardly believe my good luck. My father was sitting in the kitchen for his afternoon coffee break, a cup of coffee and a piece of cake on the table in front of him. Every once in a while, Dad would be in the house when I came home from school, and today happened to be one of those days.

"Daddy!" I said, feeling somewhat breathless from hurrying to the house.

"Hi-ya, kiddo. What'd you do, run up the hill?

"Almost," I said.

"How come you're in such a rush?" Mom asked. She was sitting across the table from Dad.

I set my books on the table and threw myself into a chair.

"We watched a movie today about making maple syrup! Daddy, we have maple trees. Can we make syrup?"

Dad set down his coffee cup. "We've got the wrong kind of trees. You need sugar maples—and we have silver maples."

"I know that," I said. "But the guy in the movie said…"

"Said what?" Mom asked.

"He said that all maple trees have sweet sap."

"All maple trees *do* have sweet sap, but sugar maples make the best syrup," Dad said.

"I know. That's what they said in the movie, too, but—can't we try?"

Dad chewed a forkful of cake and then washed it down with a swallow of coffee. Mom had made a yellow cake. When Mom baked a cake, she made either white, yellow or chocolate. She said we went through cake so fast she'd rather not spend extra time making anything fancy like red devil's food layer cake or German chocolate or spice oatmeal, although sometimes she baked a marble cake or a pineapple upside-down cake.

"I suppose there's no harm in trying to make some syrup," Dad said as he put his coffee cup on the table. "In fact, it might be kind of fun to see what happens."

"I think it would be fun to try, too," Mom said.

I looked back and forth between Mom and Dad.

"Daddy! Do you mean it?"

My father reached for his coffee cup. "Sure. In fact, I noticed a little bit of sap dripping today…so…what say we get started right now? I've got time before I have to feed the cows."

"Change your clothes first, young lady," Mom said. "I know what kind of messes you can get into sometimes."

I went upstairs to change out of my school clothes, and when I came back downstairs, I put on my coat and hat and mittens. It was not terribly cold outside, but the wind was chilly. Dad had already put on his coat and cap, and together we went to the machine shed where he rummaged around on the workbench until he found what he was looking for—a short piece of narrow pipe.

"What's that for?" I asked.

"This," Dad said, holding up the pipe, "is going to be our tap."

The pipe was about as big around as the end of Dad's finger.

My father reached for a hammer and headed out the door toward the silver maple tree across the driveway from the machine shed. Needles had followed us to the machine shed, and as we crossed the driveway, he followed us to the maple tree and sat down not far from Dad's feet.

"I think this tree is the best," Dad said, "because it's close to the house and you don't have to wade through the snow to get to it."

The other maple trees grew along the edge of the yard, and getting to them would mean walking through the two feet of snow on the ground.

"Let's see," Dad said, gazing at the trunk of the tree, "we don't want it too low and we don't want it too high."

The silver maple across the driveway from the machine shed was so big that I could not even begin to put my arms around it. On the side opposite the gas barrel, Dad had built a tree house for me a few years ago. The tree house was nothing more than an old barn door nailed up as a platform with a railing around the outside, but I enjoyed stretching out in my tree house in the shade of the silver maple on a hot summer day with one or two of the barn cats to keep me company.

"What about right here?" Dad said, pointing to a spot about three feet off the ground. "When it's time to dump the bucket of sap, you'll be able to lift it off there."

Dad put the pipe against the light gray bark and began tapping with the hammer. "I don't want to hit it too hard," he said, "because I don't want the pipe to break. I might not have another one this size."

After a few more taps he stopped and turned to me. "While I'm doing this, why don't you go to the barn and get a calf bucket. Take it to the milkhouse and scrub it out good and then bring it here."

The sound of the metallic *chink-chink-chink-chink* of Dad tapping on the pipe followed me to the barn, and when I came back out a few minutes later with a calf pail, Dad was still carefully tapping the pipe. I went into the milkhouse, dumped some soap into the bucket, turned on the hot water and scrubbed it with the green scratchy pad we used to wash the milkers. I dumped the soapy water down the drain and rinsed the pail, first with hot water and then with cold until I was sure all of the soap had been rinsed out. Making sure the soap was rinsed off was an important part of washing the milkers, and I figured it would be important for maple syrup, too.

I returned to the maple tree with the clean pail, and Dad had finished tapping and was standing back, watching the pipe. Needles still sat by Dad's feet. Clear fluid slowly dripped out the end of the pipe, and it looked like what I had seen in the movie. One drop would come out of the pipe, and then a little while later, another drop would drip out of the pipe.

Dad caught a drop of the fluid on his finger, tasted it and nodded. "This'll do, I think. Wanna taste it?"

I put my finger under the pipe. The drop felt cold, like a drop of water from the tap, and when I tasted it, I was surprised to find that it tasted like weak sugar water, as if someone had mixed a teaspoon of sugar into a gallon of water.

Dad picked up the pail and hung it from the pipe. "The sap's not running very fast now," he said, "but as the weather warms up, the sap will run faster."

"How often do I have to dump that?" I asked.

"Every day," Dad said. "Check it every day when you come home from school."

"How many gallons of syrup will we make?" I asked.

Dad lifted off his blue-and-white pin-striped chore cap and settled it back on his head. "Gallons? We'll be lucky to get a cup of syrup when we're done."

A cup?

I tilted my head back and stared at the tree branches arching high overhead. The tree was much taller than the white garage and the small round granary next to it, and surely a tree this big could produce enough sap for more than a cup of syrup.

My father must have known what I was thinking. "When you cook the sap, the water evaporates, so to make even a quart of syrup, it would probably take more sap than we'll get from this tree."

"But…if we're only going to make a cup, how many days will I have to dump the pail?"

Dad shook his head. "Days? It'll be more like weeks."

"Weeks?" I said. "It will take *weeks* to fill the kettle Mom said we could use?"

My mother had found an old kettle in the cupboard that she rarely used and said I could put the maple sap in the kettle.

"Sap'll be running for a couple of weeks. I don't know if we'll get enough to fill the kettle, but yes, it's going to take that long to get enough to make a little syrup," Dad replied.

We watched for a few minutes as the sap slowly dripped out of the pipe, and then Dad, Needles and I went to the barn to feed the cows.

The next day when I arrived home from school, I checked the pail before I even went into the house. The calf pail had an inch of clear fluid in the bottom. Needles came to see what I was doing, and when he concluded it wasn't anything very interesting, he went back to a small spot of brown grass by the machine shed where the snow had melted and settled down in the sun with a happy sigh. I took the pail off the pipe, carried it to the house, dumped it into the kettle and went back outside to hang it on the pipe again.

"You should put that in the refrigerator," Mom said when I returned to the kitchen. She pulled open the drawer under the stove, searched among the lids and held one up. "Put a cover on it, too," she said, handing the cover to me.

I checked the calf pail every day for the next few weeks. Some days the pail held more sap and some days less. Dad said the amount of sap was related to how warm the temperature got during the day and how cold the temperature dropped at night.

Then one day when I checked the pail, I discovered only a small amount of sap in the bottom—and saw that no more sap was dripping from the pipe. I went to the barn to ask Dad about it, and he said it meant the sap had stopped running for the year.

I hurried into the house to tell my mother the sap was finished.

"When can we make syrup?" I asked as I dumped the last few drops of sap into the kettle.

Mom was brushing shortening on hot loaves of bread she had taken out of the oven. "What about Saturday?" she said.

Saturday was three days away.

"Saturday? Why can't we do it now?" I asked.

"Because it will more than likely take all day," Mom said.

"*All* day?" I said.

"Yes," she replied. "All day. It's going to take a while to boil down that much liquid until it's thick enough for syrup."

First thing Saturday morning after I came in the house from carrying milk to the milkhouse for Dad and feeding calves, I took the kettle out of the refrigerator and set it on the stove.

Mom was sitting by the table with a cup of coffee. "Turn the burner onto medium-high for a few minutes until it starts to boil, and then we're going to turn it down far enough just so it simmers or is not quite simmering," she said.

For the rest of the day—in between helping Loretta with the cleaning and riding Dusty around the driveway (being careful to stay off the lawn because where the snow had melted the lawn was soft, and Mom said she didn't want hoof prints in the lawn) and working on my Sunday school lesson for the next day and finishing up some arithmetic homework—I kept checking the kettle to see how much of the water had boiled away. At first, after an hour of cooking, I couldn't see much difference, although by afternoon, half the liquid had evaporated. In the evening, when we came in the house after the chores were finished, Mom said the syrup was done.

"This isn't very thick," I said, stirring the contents of the kettle with the straight-edged metal spoon that had been a Christmas gift from our milk hauler a few years ago.

"No, it's not," Mom replied. "But it's not going to be as thick as pancake syrup you can buy, either."

"It's a nice color, though," Loretta said.

The syrup was a pale caramel color that looked—well—that looked good enough to eat.

"Should we taste it?" Mom asked.

I thought for a bit and shook my head. "I want to wait and see what it tastes like on pancakes," I said.

"I guess that way, it would be a surprise for all of us, wouldn't it," Loretta said.

"How much syrup did we end up with?" Dad asked.

"I don't know," Mom said. She looked at me. "Pour it in a pint jar and find out."

I reached into the cupboard for an empty pint jar, and Loretta helped me carefully pour the syrup into the jar. We had many pint jars because Mom used them to make jam and jelly, and we finished off a pint every week or two. After a half a dozen jars had accumulated in the cupboard, Mom would tell me to take them to the basement and put them on the shelf with the other empty jars.

When the last of the syrup had dripped into the jar, I discovered Dad was wrong.

We did not end up with one cup of syrup.

There were two cups.

The pint jar was full.

"Two cups!" Dad said. "I'm surprised."

"When can we have pancakes?" I asked.

"How about tomorrow for breakfast?" Mom suggested.

The next day when we came in the house after doing the morning milking, Dad made pancakes. I watched as he measured out the ingredients, stirred the batter with the wire whisk, dropped spoonfuls of batter onto the hot griddle and let them bake until bubbles appeared on one side. Then he flipped them over and let them bake on the other side. He repeated the process until there was an entire stack of golden brown pancakes.

Dad set the plate of pancakes on the table. "Dig in," he said, as he pulled out his chair.

Mom took one pancake, Loretta took one, I helped myself to three, and Dad put four on his plate. Ingman was upstairs sleeping. He had worked the nightshift at the creamery and would have to taste the maple syrup later.

"Well, what do you think?" Mom asked.

"Delicious!" Loretta said.

"Not bad," Dad said. "It's thinner than what we had at the lumber camp, and not quite as maple-y, but it's got a good flavor."

I was too busy chewing to say a single word.

Even though the syrup was not as thick and rich as the maple syrup Dad remembered from when he was a kid, at least I was able to determine one thing about maple syrup. And it was the most important thing of all.

Maple syrup, I found out, tasted every bit as good on pancakes as I had always imagined.

****

~ 20 ~
Cream of the Crop

I looked across the supper table at my friends from school. Neither of them lived on a farm, so I hoped they wouldn't be too disappointed. Now that they were actually here for a slumber party, I realized there wasn't much to do on a farm. Not in early spring when it was muddy outside and still cold. And not like in town, where you could walk to the store for candy bars, or go ice skating on the little pond by Main Street, or go to the restaurant for a hamburger and chocolate milk, or if it was a Friday evening in the fall or the winter, walk to school to see a football game or a basketball game. I did not know these things from personal experience, but I had heard other girls in our class talking about slumber parties they had been to, and when they told of going to the store or the restaurant or the skating pond or to school to watch a game, they laughed and giggled and said they'd had the best time in the whole wide world.

The only thing I could offer at my slumber party was going out to the barn with Dad after supper. When we arrived home from school, I had wanted to get Dusty ready so we could ride her, but Mom said I could not, because Dad was busy feeding the cows, and since the other girls had never ridden a pony all by themselves, she was afraid that without an adult to supervise, someone would get hurt.

But, when I thought about taking my friends out to the barn after supper, it seemed to me that the barn was not the best of places. For one thing, it was ripe with the smell of cow manure, even if Dad had cleaned it during the day, and for another thing, it was grimy with hay chaff and feed dust and the chalky grittiness of the white barn lime Dad sprinkled on the floor. I loved going out to the barn myself, and yet, I had also started thinking about the barn in a whole new way, thinking about it in the way I imagined people who did not have barns would think about it. Compared to a store or a restaurant or a school, the barn was smelly and dirty.

Why did I ever want to have a slumber party? The Halloween party last fall was all right because it was Halloween and because some of the girls lived on farms. We had played games and told ghost stories and had bobbed for apples in Mom's old round washpan and had ridden in the wagon behind the corn picker. But this was different. My sister had been home for the Halloween party, and she knew how to make everything fun. Tonight Loretta was at her apartment, as she always was during the week in the winter so she wouldn't have to drive back and forth every day on slippery roads, even though it was spring rather than winter. Loretta would not move home from her apartment until the end of the month.

I had invited my very best friend, Vicki, to the slumber party, too, and if Vicki was here, it would be all right because she also knew how to make everything fun. The only problem was that Vicki's mom had said she could come to the slumber party or she could come over Sunday afternoon, but that she could not do both. We talked it over, and Vicki decided she would rather come on Sunday. "We can go exploring around the creek at the bottom of the pasture. Maybe we'll see some tadpoles!" she said. I knew it was too early for tadpoles, but it wouldn't hurt to check.

At first, I had wanted to have the slumber party in February when we had plenty of snow and could go sledding as soon as we got home from school. Mom, however, had said it would be better to have the party at the end of March or early April when it was not so cold upstairs.

After my mother had pointed out how cold it was upstairs in our house during the winter, I could see what she was getting at. I slept under several layers of blankets and quilts, but I supposed my friends' bedrooms probably wouldn't be as cold. Our house had been built before 1900, so the upstairs bedrooms did not have any heat ducts, and Mom said I would be a poor hostess if I expected my friends to sleep upstairs in the middle of winter.

Unfortunately, it was too late to cancel the slumber party. My friends were here, and we were getting ready to eat supper, as soon as my mother finished dishing up the food and sat down at the table.

"Would anyone like a glass of milk?" Mom asked. She leaned on the stove for support. The stove was halfway between the refrigerator and the cupboard by the sink where we kept the glasses.

"Yes, please," said one of my friends.

"Me, too," said the other.

I didn't say anything because I knew my mother was not asking me if I wanted a glass of milk. I wasn't 'company'—I would get a glass of milk one way or the other.

My mother let go of the stove, grasped the back of her chair, opened the refrigerator door and reached for a pitcher of milk. She set it on the stove, made her way to the utensil drawer, pulled out a long-handled spoon and began stirring the milk.

"Why are you mixing the milk?" asked one of the girls.

"Because of the cream," my mother said.

"Cream?"

"The cream rises to the top, so we have to stir it back in," Dad explained.

"Cream comes from milk?" the other girl asked.

I looked at her with a feeling of surprise. How could anyone not know that cream came from milk?

"We always get cream from the store," one of the girls explained.

"How come store milk doesn't have cream on the top?" asked the other.

"Because it's homogenized," Mom said.

"Hum-aj-ah-what?"

"Homogenized. That means it's been stirred by a special process so the cream can't rise to the top like it does with our milk," Mom explained.

"Can you see the cream? Before you stir it up?" asked the girl who had trouble saying 'homogenized.'

"You can't tell much by looking in the pitcher," Dad answered. "But after supper, we'll pour some milk into a canning jar and by tomorrow morning, you'll be able to see the layer of cream."

"Is it like real cream?" one girl asked. "I mean, when we buy cream, we use it to make whipped cream."

"This'll whip, just like any other cream," Dad said.

Mom finished pouring the milk into glasses. "Roy, when was the last time you turned the bulk tank on?"

A few years ago, we had switched from using milk cans to keeping our milk in a stainless steel tank. The tank had a big paddle in the middle that stirred the milk and kept it cool. The milk hauler came every other day to pick up the load of milk, and he would be arriving again tomorrow morning. I knew the milk hauler would be coming tomorrow because this morning, when I carried milk for Dad before getting ready for school, the bulk tank had been almost half full.

Dad frowned as he considered my mother's question concerning the last time he had turned on the bulk tank agitator. I liked knowing that the paddle was called an agitator. Mom said that the word 'agitate' meant to keep something stirred up. During the winter and even in early spring before the weather grew warmer, my father didn't leave the agitator on all of the time, otherwise the milk tended to freeze.

"Hmmm..." he said, "the last time I stirred the milk was about noon, I guess."

"Well, before you start milking tonight, would you please take a jar with you and get some cream?"

I turned to look at my mother, who had sat down in her chair, twisted herself around to face the table and was using her hands to place her legs in a more comfortable position. Sitting down by the table, Mom said, was one of things that people who did not have polio took for granted.

"Why does Dad have to get cream?" I asked.

"Oh," she said casually, "I thought maybe while you girls were in the barn, I could make some Jell-O. I'll set it in the freezer for a bit. Then when you come in, we'll make whipped cream."

"Whipped cream!" said one of the girls. "I *love* whipped cream."

"Me, too! Me, too!" the other girl chimed in.

My mother smiled. "Then whipped cream we shall have."

"We don't get whipped cream very often at home," one girl said.

"Us, either," the other girl said. "Mostly just at Thanksgiving or Christmas or Easter."

"You only have whipped cream at Thanksgiving, Christmas or Easter?" I said.

"And maybe one or two other times, like if it's somebody's birthday," one girl said.

While it was true that we did not make whipped cream every day, we often had whipped cream three or four times a month. If Loretta baked a pie or made those little cookies in the waffle maker, or Mom made gingerbread or pound cake or pineapple upside-down cake or bread pudding—or Loretta brought home bananas and ice cream and maraschino cherries to make banana splits—we made whipped cream.

"I'll get some cream before I start putting the milkers together," Dad said. "And then you girls can bring it back to the house."

"Goody," said one of my friends. "We're going to have whipped cream!"

For supper, Mom had made round steak and mashed potatoes and gravy, and when we were finished eating, my friends and I put on our coats and went to the milkhouse with Dad and watched while he filled a quart jar half full of cream. He set another empty jar on top of the rack where the milkers were put to dry and said that after he was done milking, he would fill the second jar with milk so my friends could see the cream at the top when we got up in the morning.

"Look at all the milk!" one girl said as she peered down into the bulk tank.

Dad had lifted the cover and propped it up so he could more easily skim off some cream.

"It will be almost full by the time we're finished milking tomorrow morning," Dad said.

"Full!" my friend replied.

"I've never seen so much milk," said the other girl.

Dad skimmed off another dipper of cream and poured it in the jar. The thick cream coated the outside of the aluminum dipper.

"This is just a small bulk tank," Dad said.

"A small one?"

"Farmers who milk forty or fifty cows have a lot bigger bulk tanks than this. We only milk twenty cows."

"Twenty!" the other girl said. "I've never even been close to a cow."

"Well," Dad said as he skimmed another dipper of cream out of the bulk tank, " you'll see twenty of 'em pretty quick here."

My father finished skimming the cream, handed the jar to me, and we took the jar to the house. Or I should say, we *took turns* carrying the jar to the house. Each of the girls wanted to have a chance to carry the cream.

Just as all three of us marched into the kitchen, my mother poured boiling water over the dry Jell-O she had dumped into a bowl. The sweet scent of strawberries instantly filled the air.

Two empty boxes of strawberry Jell-O sat on the counter.

"Strawberry is my favorite," one girl said.

"Strawberry is my favorite, too," Mom replied.

We stayed in the kitchen while Mom poured cold water into the Jell-O. She stirred the contents of the bowl and then asked me to set the bowl in the freezer for her. I knew that carrying a bowl of liquid across the kitchen to the refrigerator—even though it was only a short distance—was difficult for her because she had to hold onto the counter or a kitchen chair with one hand while she carried the bowl with the other. Taking the bowl out of the freezer would be much easier because all she would have to do is switch the bowl from one spot to the other.

I put the bowl in the freezer and shut the door.

"Come on," I said. "Let's go out to the barn."

We headed through the porch and went down the steps single file. The sky was growing dark, and a few stars were beginning to twinkle. I could hear the *chuff-chuff-chuff* of the milker pump. Dad had already started milking.

"What's that noise?" one of the girls asked as we walked across the yard toward the barn.

"What noise?"

"The puffing noise."

"That's the milker pump," I said.

"What does it do?"

"It runs the milking machines," I explained.

"How does it do that?"

"You'll see when we get into the barn," I said.

Less than a minute later, I opened the barn door, and once again, I was surrounded by the familiar smell of cows. Dad was milking on the far end of the barn. He always started milking on the other end. My friends spent a long time watching the milking machines and listening to the swish-swish of the vacuum line.

"*That's* where milk comes from?" one girl said.

"This is it," Dad said. He shut off the valve on the milker, carried the milker into the center aisle and took off the cover.

"Is that all from one cow?" the other girl asked.

"Actually," Dad replied, "it's two cows, but there're a couple that can almost fill a bucket themselves."

My friends turned to look at the cows standing side by side up and down the barn aisle.

"How can they make so much milk in—what's that thing called?"

"It's called an udder," I said.

"They make milk so they can feed their calves," Dad explained. "But we feed their calves for them, and then we sell the milk."

"What do you feed the calves?" one of my friends asked.

"Milk replacer," I said.

"That's powdered milk you mix with water," Dad explained. "We start out with milk replacer when they're little, and when they get older, like most of 'em are now, we give them some cow feed, too, and some hay."

"Are we going to feed the calves tonight?" one girl asked.

"Of course," Dad said. "They have to eat, just like everybody else."

"Goody! We're going to feed the calves," she said.

As Dad worked his way down the barn aisle with the milkers, and in between carrying milk to the milkhouse, my friends and I played with Needles, who performed his trick of climbing up on the milk stool and sitting, prim and proper, with his tail hanging almost to the floor while we brushed him with Dusty's curry comb. We also visited my favorite cows, petted the barn cats, fed the calves, explored the haymow and when the milking was done, we helped Dad feed hay.

"This is fun!" one girl said, enthusiastically shaking out a flake of hay for the cow in front of her. Hay chaff flew in all directions, and the cow ended up with a few wisps of hay dangling from her ears.

"The whole thing is fun!" the other girl said. "But I really liked feeding the calves. I didn't know anything could drink so fast."

Although there had been some light in the sky when we went to the barn, by the time we came out of the barn, it was completely dark. In another month, Dad said it would still be light outside when we finished milking, and I could hardly wait because that would mean it would truly be spring.

"Do you think the Jell-O is ready?" Dad asked as we walked toward the house.

"I hope so," one of the girls said. "I'm starving! I didn't know going out to the barn was so much work."

In the glow of the yard light, which we turned on in the fall, winter and early spring when we went out to the barn and turned off when we came back from the barn, I could see my father biting his lips and trying not to smile.

Dad and I took off our coats and boots in the porch, but my guests took off their coats in the kitchen. They had brought old clothes to wear to the barn, and while they were folding up their coats and putting them in paper grocery bags, my mother made her way into the kitchen from the living room and sat down at her end of the table.

"Wash your hands," Mom said, "and then you can make the whipped cream."

"You know how to make whipped cream *all by yourself?*" one of my friends said.

I was tempted to say that, yes, I knew how to make whipped cream all by myself, except the truth of the matter was, when I made whipped cream either Mom or Loretta would keep an eye on it so they could tell me when to shut off the mixer.

"Sort of," I said. "Mom or my big sister tells me when it's time to stop mixing it."

"Wow," said one of the girls. "You get to make whipped cream all by yourself! Mom won't even let me hold the mixer."

One by one, we took turns at the bathroom sink, washing our hands with a bar of Ivory soap. Mom said I should let company go first whenever we had company, so I was the last one to wash my hands. When I was finished, I hung up the towel, went to the kitchen, reached into the cupboard for a mixing bowl, and then I got the jar of cream out of the refrigerator. Mom had already set the mixer on the cupboard and had put the beaters into the little holes where they belonged and had plugged in the mixer.

Soon my friends and I were taking turns holding the mixer as it whipped the cream, and when the cream started to thicken, we took turns pouring in the sugar while one of us held the mixer.

"Let me see it," Mom said after a while.

I set the mixer on end and took the bowl and a spoon over to her. My mother dabbed the spoon into the bowl a couple of times.

"Another minute or so, and it will be done," she said.

"Yipeeee!" one of the girls said. "We've almost got whipped cream!"

A little while later we all sat around the table with bowls of strawberry Jell-O covered in generous dollops of whipped cream.

"How does it taste?" Mom asked.

"Yummmmmy!" said one girl.

"Wait 'til I tell everybody at school we made *real* whipped cream! That came from *real* cows. And that we made it all by ourselves!" declared the other.

"Well, not *all* by ourselves," the first girl said. "Mrs. Ralph helped us."

"And we got to pet the cows that made the cream!" exclaimed the other girl. "I've never petted cows before. I never knew cows made cream!"

My mother smiled. Then Dad caught my eye and winked.

I had started out so afraid it would be a boring slumber party. Who would have ever figured we could have so much fun eating 'real' whipped cream? Or petting the cows who made the cream?

And we didn't even have to go anywhere to do it. Not to a store or a restaurant or to school—or even to the pond by Main Street.

****

~ Acknowledgements ~

Thank you to my husband, Randy Simpson, who, after three books, continues to say he is my biggest fan. Randy also is my website designer, my business partner, my administrative assistant, my book cover designer—and the person who tells me to keep going on those days when I feel like giving up.

And, as I always say, thank you to my readers, because without readers, writers wouldn't have a job!

****

~ How to Order More Books ~

Here's how to order more copies of *Cream of the Crop, Give Me a Home Where the Dairy Cows Roam* and *Christmas in Dairyland:*

- Order on the Internet through Booklocker.com
- Order on the Internet through Amazon.com or Barnes & Noble.
- Order through your local bookstore.
- Call LeAnn at (715) 962-3368.
- Write to LeAnn at E6689 970th Ave.; Colfax, WI 54730
- Order from LeAnn's website—www.ruralroute2.com

When you order books directly from the author (either by calling, writing or ordering through www.ruralroute2.com), you can request autographed copies with personalized inscriptions. And no need to pre-pay. An invoice will be sent with your order.

****

Autographed books make great gifts for Christmas, birthdays, graduations, and other special occasions!

****

~ Book Review ~

Give Me a Home Where the Dairy Cows Roam
(Oct. 2004; ISBN-1-59113-592-3; $13.95; http://ruralroute2.com)

Give Me A Home Where The Dairy Cows Roam is a collection of autobiographical stories drawn from author LeAnn Ralph's family dairy farm in Wisconsin in a time when small family farms were commonplace in the Badger State's rural countryside. Now that we live in a time when approximately 85% of American family dairy farms have disappeared into suburban township developments or absorbed into agribusiness scale corporate farming enclaves, LeAnn takes us back some forty years ago into an era when dairy farming was a dawn-to-dusk life, seven days a week lifestyle that bonded parents and children with hard work and a sense of the land, animals, and homestead that is rapidly passing from today's expanding urban society.

More than just an autobiographical collection of anecdotal stories, *Give Me A Home Where The Dairy Cows Roam* is also enhanced with a recipe for making homemade ice cream without an ice cream maker and a recipe for "Norma's Homemade Bread". Highly recommended reading, *Give Me A Home Where The Dairy Cows Roam* should be on the shelves of every community library in Wisconsin.

James A. Cox, Editor-in-Chief
Midwest Book Review

****

~ Book Review ~

Christmas in Dairyland (True Stories from a Wisconsin Farm)
(August 2003; ISBN 1-59113-366-1; $13.95; http://ruralroute2.com)

Christmas In Dairyland: True Stories From A Wisconsin Farm by
LeAnn R. Ralph is a heartwarming anthology of true anecdotes of rural
life on a Wisconsin dairy farm. Even though Wisconsin is still known
as America's Dairyland, life on a family homestead is fast being
replaced by corporate agribusiness, and the memories treasured in
Christmas In Dairyland are quickly becoming unique milestones of an
era needing to be preserved in thought and print for the sake of future
generations. *Christmas In Dairyland* is simply wonderful reading and is
a "must" for all Wisconsin public library collections.

James A. Cox, Editor-in-Chief
Midwest Book Review

****

~ About the Author ~

LeAnn R. Ralph earned an undergraduate degree in English with a writing emphasis from the University of Wisconsin-Whitewater and also earned a Master of Arts in Teaching from UW-Whitewater. She worked as a newspaper reporter for nine years, has taught English at a boys' boarding school, has worked as a substitute teacher and a parish secretary, and is the former editor of the *Wisconsin Regional Writer* (the quarterly publication of the Wisconsin Regional Writers' Assoc.).

The author lives in rural Wisconsin with her husband, two dogs, two horses and assorted cats and is working on her next book, *Where the Green Grass Grows*, another collection of true stories.

If you would like to receive notification when LeAnn's next book is available, write to her at E6689 970th Ave., Colfax, WI 54730, or e-mail her at — bigpines@ruralroute2.com

In addition to *Cream of the Crop*, LeAnn is the author of the books, *Give Me a Home Where the Dairy Cows Roam* (trade paperback; September 2004; $13.95); *Christmas in Dairyland (True Stories from a Wisconsin Farm)* (trade paperback; August 2003; $13.95) and *Preserve Your Family History (A Step-by-Step Guide for Writing Oral Histories)* (e-book; April 2004; $7.95).

****

~ About the Book Cover ~

The picture on the front cover is of a Jersey calf born in our barn. We had one Jersey cow (named—what else?—Jersey), and I really appreciated her petite calves because even I could pick them up and carry them right after they were born. The Holstein calves were much too big and too heavy for me to carry.

The aerial photo of our farm on the back cover was taken sometime during the mid-1960s. To determine whether the photo was a copyrighted photo, I took the picture out of the frame. On the back of the cardboard was stamped "National Air Photo's Co., Bloomer, Wis." but there was nothing on the picture itself to indicate a copyright.

Years ago, Wisconsin had 50,000 more dairy farms than it has today, and a number of aerial photographers went around and took pictures of farms and then asked farmers if they wanted to buy those pictures. But, as the dairy farms disappeared, so did the aerial photo companies.

As I understand it, according to the copyright law in effect at that time, the picture would have had to have a copyright symbol, the name of the photographer and the year on the photo itself to be copyrighted. After a fruitless search on the Internet for information about the company, I finally thought of calling the newspaper in Bloomer.

The lady at the newspaper was extremely helpful. She made a phone call and then called me back (within five minutes!) with the name and telephone number of the son of the man who had taken the photo. I told her why I wanted more information about the picture, and she said that the company was no longer in existence, that the photographer, whose name was William Barthen, was deceased, and that she doubted those kinds of pictures had been copyrighted.

I was able to reach the photographer's son by telephone the next morning. He said that the pictures taken by his father were not copyrighted, and that in any case, "it makes no difference to me if you use it."

The picture of my pony, Dusty, was taken in the barn at some point before she got her haircut because of the cockleburs.

The picture of Randy and I and Pixie and Charlie is a "self portrait." Brilliant man that he is, my husband wondered if our digital camera would fit on the tripod for the video camera. It did! He set up camera on the tripod and then figured out how to use the timer. He set the timer and then hot-footed it over to the 'rock table' we have in our yard where I was sitting, composed himself and waited for the timer to go off. Of course, it was not a matter of going through this process once and ending up with a good picture. We repeated the process many times before we got a couple of good pictures. Pixie and Charlie thought it was some kind of game and enjoyed themselves tremendously.

****